# Vancouver

Footprint

*Matthew Gardner and Alison Bigg*

# Contents

**Listings**

# About the authors

Matthew Gardner grew up in London, gaining a French degree from Bristol University and a teaching diploma from Goldsmith College. After two years as a French teacher, he left to write a novel, but caught the travel bug instead. He has spent most of the last eight years travelling, particularly in Latin America, Asia and Canada, and has written several travel guides. His main passions are music and movies, literature and landscapes, football and food. Alison Bigg grew up in various parts of Africa, the Middle East and Canada, and has lived for many years in Vancouver and Victoria. She studied Fine Arts and photography at Emily Carr College of Art and Design in Vancouver. To research this and Footprint's Western Canada Handbook, Matthew and Alison spent seven months on the road, covering about 20,000 miles in a van with their dog, Lola.

# Acknowledgements

Matthew and Alison would like to thank: Kathy and Skip, Holly and Kristen, and the whole Read clan; Laura Serena at Tourism Vancouver for the loan of some very useful books; Tessa and Adam for help with tricky Whistler; Stephen for help with the Gay and lesbian section; Sam for the contact, and for being Sam; Sara for help with the Art and architecture section; and mostly Felicity for whipping us into shape in the nicest possible way.

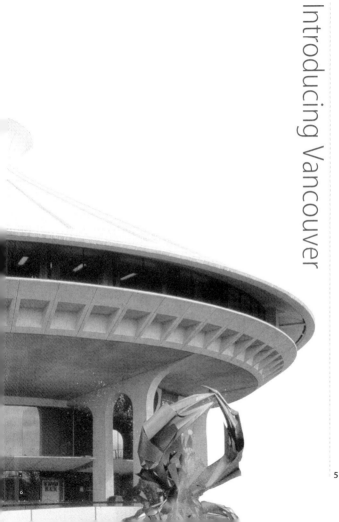

Introducing Vancouver

One of the world's youngest cities, Vancouver is also among the most modern and rapidly developing. Sleek state-of-the-art glass towers are interspersed with the odd Gothic church, Victorian warehouse, art deco confection and other more unusual constructions strangely reminiscent of a sailing ship, the Colosseum, a silver golf-ball, a giant marshmallow... This delightfully eclectic cityscape is utterly upstaged by its sublime location. Snow-capped mountains tower over the city, providing a breathtaking backdrop. Beaches, seawalls and ferry-buses are part of everyday life in Vancouver, which is built where river meets ocean and dissected by fjord-like inlets. And the frequent rain, along with a surprisingly mild climate, feeds a whole host of flower gardens and some of the planet's biggest trees.

## Lotus land

Closer to Japan than it is to Britain – a third of the residents are of Asian origin – Vancouver is a genuine meeting place of East and West. Nicknamed 'lotus land', Vancouver actually runs the whole cosmopolitan gamut, resulting in a fascinating array of distinctive, starkly contrasting neighbourhoods. Here before them all were Canada's First Nations, whose exquisite carvings and totem poles represent the city's most unmissable cultural experience. Vancouver's rare cultural symbiosis informs every aspect of life, from people to street signs to festivals and the city's extraordinarily diverse and competitive culinary scene.

## Granola culture

East Coasters think of British Columbians as tree-huggers and granola eaters, mocking a West Coast vibe that makes Vancouver more comparable to San Francisco than Toronto. The air and streets are shockingly clean and crime rates are low. Vancouver's population smokes less, reads more, drinks more wine, eats out more and buys more sporting equipment than people in other Canadian cities. Health-conscious, polite and relaxed, Vancouverites tend to be politically liberal and opposed to the corporate culture. After all Greenpeace was founded here.

## Convivial pursuits

Living in an area of outstanding natural beauty, British Columbians are crazy about outdoor pursuits. Consequently, Vancouver and its surrounding areas offer a staggering range of activities catering for beginners and experts alike. There are three ski-hills right in town, plus excellent mountain biking and gorgeous hikes to dizzying panoramas; and the continent's number one ski resort is just two hours north. On the way are mountain trails and landscapes to rival even the Rockies, as well as the country's best climbing, wind-surfing and bald eagle-watching. And, what's more, local waters offer first-class kayaking, sailing, scuba diving, surfing and whale-watching.

# At a glance

## Downtown and Yaletown

Bristling with energy, Vancouver's Downtown peninsula is relatively tiny, yet contains several distinct neighbourhoods and the lion's share of the sights. This is where you'll find the tallest buildings, the most exclusive boutiques and the fanciest restaurants, as well as the pick of Vancouver's culture and nightlife and a busy, multicultural throng of human activity. A jamboree bag of architectural styles that includes many of the city's finest structures, coupled with the perpetual mountain and water views, makes for fascinating strolling.

South of the city centre, you can skirt the distinctive air-supported dome of BC Place, and the Colosseum-like Public Library, before hitting Yaletown. The massive, old red-brick buildings of this former warehouse district are steadily being converted into spacious apartments and trendy bars and restaurants, frequented by the city's young and upwardly mobile. Many walk a thin line between panache and pretentiousness, and the whole zone needs time to mellow into a genuine sense of style, but it's a fascinating area. West of here is the sleazy southern end of Granville Street, which leads back to the centre.

## Gastown, East Side and Chinatown

To the northeast of the city centre is Gastown, Vancouver's oldest quarter and a jumble of contradictions. While the restored cobblestone streets, Victorian mews and red-brick buildings are undeniably quaint, the effect is ruined by a gaggle of tacky souvenir shops, then redeemed by some excellent galleries, antique stores and First Nations art boutiques, as well as Vancouver's hippest nightclub scene. Immediately adjacent is the sleazy and derelict East Side, home to Vancouver's down-and-outs, prostitutes, drug-dealers and seedy pawn shops, yet grimly fascinating and possessing a few outstanding buildings and the last surviving examples of once-prevalent neon. South of here is another world again, the big and bustling Chinatown, its streets overflowing with baskets of outlandish produce and aromatic restaurants whose windows display lacquered ducks, slabs of barbecued pork, and plastic replicas of eerily familiar dishes. This is the neck of the peninsula, sandwiched between False Creek to the south with the futuristic silver sphere of Science World and Burrard Inlet to the north.

## West End and Stanley Park
The broad and perpetually vibrant urban zone that occupies most of the peninsula's western half is known as the West End. This is Canada's most densely populated area, half of whose inhabitants are aged between 20 and 40, among them Western Canada's largest gay community. A vibrant neighbourhood atmosphere makes Denman Street and Davie Street two of the best zones for restaurants, bars and people-watching. The tip of the peninsula is entirely occupied by Stanley Park, Canada's largest urban park. A popular 9-km seawall follows its circumference past beaches and viewpoints, while trails criss-cross its interior. As well as the famous giant trees, the park has a fine aquarium, rhododendron and rose gardens, two restaurants, an open-air theatre, a miniature railway, and a stand of totem poles.

## Granville Island and Vanier Park
Granville Bridge leads south from the downtown peninsula to Granville Island, Vancouver's Covent Garden but in a maritime setting. Clustered together are a wonderful food market, countless galleries and studios selling arts and crafts, a handful of theatres and restaurants, an art school, boat repair shops and a first-class museum. You can walk west along the water from here to Vanier Park, home of three key museums.

## Kitsilano and Point Grey

The very popular Kits Beach marks the edge of Kitsilano. Once the focus of Vancouver's counter-culture, the neighbourhood has been taken over by yuppies, with an upmarket yet alternative atmosphere. Sections of 4th Avenue and 9th Avenue offer some of Vancouver's best shopping, strolling and restaurants. Further west are Point Grey and the city university, several excellent beaches, a couple of fine botanical gardens, and the city's number one sight, the UBC Museum of Anthropology.

## South and East Vancouver

The remainder of South Vancouver is distinguished only by a handful of lovely parks and gardens. In the east, however, close to Downtown, are two of the most interesting neighbourhoods. Commercial Drive, once known as Little Italy, is a cosmopolitan, bohemian area, with bags of character and plenty to eat, drink and observe. Moving in the same direction, and maybe even more real, is Main Street south of 6th Avenue, where trendy but gritty little cafés and restaurants compliment a wealth of antique and second-hand stores. Further south on Main between 48th and 50th Avenues is Indiatown, alias the Punjabi Market. And beyond, at the southwestern tip of the dull suburb of Richmond, is Steveston, which has been a fishing village for over a century and still boasts the largest commercial fishing fleet on Canada's Pacific shore.

## North Shore

Across Burrard Inlet from Stanley Park's northern tip, Lion's Gate Bridge leads to the North Shore and a string of huge semi-wilderness parks and canyons that head up into the mountains, great for hiking, skiing, giant trees and sweeping views. At its western end, a short ferry ride leads to Bowen Island, an easy taste of the laid-back pace on the Gulf Islands, and one of the best day hikes in the area. At its western end is the picturesque village of Deep Cove, with the city's best kayak route and neighbourhood pub.

## Ten of the best

1 **UBC Museum of Anthropology** Pit your attention span against a mind-blowing collection of artefacts, or head straight for the superb Native West Coast carvings, p56.

2 **Chinatown** Soak up sights and smells, sample the most authentic cuisine this side of Hong Kong and learn about Taoist symbolism at the classical Chinese garden, p43.

3 **Stanley Park** Stroll past flowers, giant trees and totem poles or join locals in a ritual circuit of the seawall and meet a pair of graceful white beluga whales in the Aquarium, p48.

4 **Gastown** Wander through quaint cobblestone streets, tour First Nations art galleries, antique shops and funky retro boutiques, then head to one of the hip bars or clubs, p41.

5 **Commercial Drive** Sip strong coffee and people-watch from the patio of one of the cafés and get to know Vancouver's most bohemian, cosmopolitan neighbourhood, p62.

6 **Granville Island** Shop for innovative crafts in a warren of galleries; drool over mouthwatering foods and admire the Public Market, then saunter along False Creek to Vanier Park and the popular Kits Beach, p49.

7 **Queen Elizabeth Park** Enjoy dinner or brunch at the Seasons in the Park and savour one of the city's best views, p143.

8 **Deep Cove** Hire a kayak and take a paddle through the semi-wilderness landscapes of Indian Arm. Then choose your beer at the Raven Pub, p73.

9 **Grouse Mountain** Take the SkyRide for instant panoramic views, and then eat Pacific Northwest Native cuisine in a cedar longhouse, p69.

10 **Victoria** Spend a summer afternoon around the picturesque Inner Harbour and get a taste of the province's culture and landscapes at the Royal British Columbia Museum, p82.

# Trip planner

Vancouver is very much a year-round destination. If you like skiing or snowboarding, it's hard to beat for a short-break winter trip, when flights are at their cheapest. There are three ski-hills right in town, and Whistler, North America's biggest ski resort, is just two hours north. The prime time for skiing is March, when the days are getting longer and warmer, the snow is at its best and the restaurants and bars buzz with activity. During the mild spring season the parks explode with colour, while in autumn they adopt shades of gold and red. But Vancouver is even better in summer, when locals take to the beaches and parks, there's a constant stream of great festivals, and activities such as hiking and kayaking are at their best.

## A day

If you only have one day to spend in Vancouver, start with breakfast at *The Naam* or *Sophie's* in Kitsilano and take a bus to the UBC Museum of Anthropology, homing in on the Great Hall. Heading back to Kits, walk along the beach through Vanier Park to Granville Island. Hop on a bus to Downtown and be sure to see the Public Library, Chinatown (where you could stop for lunch) and Gastown, as you make your way to the SeaBus terminal. Cross the water to Lonsdale Quay, and catch a bus up to Grouse Mountain, for fabulous views from the SkyRide Gondola. Later, stroll down Denman Street where there are plenty of spots for dinner and drinks. Walk back into town window-shopping along Robson Street. Browse the *Georgia Strait* for a show or bar and check out the night scene in Yaletown, eventually heading back to Gastown where the best clubs are.

## A weekend

If you've got two days, explore the Downtown Peninsula on one day, and everything else on the other. Start at the waterfront and walk in an anti-clockwise loop, moving from Canada Place to the Art Gallery, BC Place, Science World, Chinatown, East Side and Gastown. *The*

*Elbow Room* is the best place for breakfast, and *Hon's Wun-Tun House* a good choice for lunch. Then follow Davie or Robson Street to Stanley Park and the Aquarium. After food and drinks on Davie or Denman Street, check out Yaletown's after-dark atmosphere on your way back to Gastown: the *Alibi Room*, *Honey Lounge* and *Lotus Club* are some of the city's most happening night-time hotspots.

Start the second day with breakfast in Kitsilano, then move on to the UBC Museum of Anthropology. Back in Kitsilano, head down to Kits Beach and along English Bay to Vanier Park. Continue on foot along False Creek to the arts and crafts Mecca of Granville Island. Grab some speciality foods from the Public Market and have a picnic by the water, then spend the rest of the afternoon exploring the North Shore. Two of the city's best restaurants, *Bishop's* and *Lumière*, are in Kitsilano, but you might prefer the more cosmopolitan and bohemian area of Commercial Drive.

If you're sticking around for a long weekend and you like mountain scenery and outdoor pursuits, head up the Sea to Sky Highway to Whistler and Garibaldi Park. Or stop at Squamish, hike to the top of the Stawamus Chief, then have a pint and lunch at the *Howe Sound Inn*. Alternatively, you could head to the laid-back Gulf Islands or to picturesque Victoria.

## A week or more

If you have a week, or money is no object, head for Tofino on Vancouver Island's rugged West Coast. The activities available here are the kind you travel for: boat trips to see thousands of migrating whales; remote hot springs; trails through stands of the oldest, biggest trees on the planet; sea-kayaking around archipelagos of scattered islands; an authentic taste of living First Nations culture; and beachcombing, surfing or storm-watching on the aptly named Long Beach.

**High lights**
*The sunlit atrium of the Public Library is spanned by elegant bridges.*

# Contemporary Vancouver

Just over a century old, Vancouver is one of the world's youngest cities; it is also one of the most thoroughly modern. In attitude it has more in common with other West Coast cities such as San Francisco than with East Coast Canadian cities like Toronto, which have retained a lingering European disposition. For quality of life Vancouver often tops the list. Where else in the world could you spend a weekend skiing, hiking in the mountains, kayaking around remote forested inlets, biking a network of tough, adrenaline-inducing trails, even scuba-diving to artificial reefs to admire the wolf eel and giant octopus, without having to cross the city limits?

The youthful, fairly wealthy and extremely cosmopolitan population, which includes a large and vibrant gay community, supports the things it loves; like restaurants. Vancouver's culinary scene is inspirational, the standard and variety astounding. The bistro, tapas or Martini bar is a Vancouver speciality, and Sunday brunch and the neighbourhood café are a municipal obsession. During one Vancouver performance, Bette Midler famously remarked: "I've never seen so much coffee in all my life. The whole town is on a caffeine jag and still nothing gets done any faster." Vancouver's cultural scene is as broad and contemporary as you'd expect of a much bigger city, with several great music venues, and theatre ranging from classics or musical blockbusters to alternative fringe pieces, a healthy smattering of repertory cinemas and art galleries running the whole gamut of styles. Vancouverites also love to shop, so expect to find all the trendy boutiques, retro clothes and speciality stores you desire.

Vancouver reveals its modernity in other ways too. Downtown is dominated by sleek glass, chrome and granite skyscrapers and almost entirely missed out on the dull and functional monstrosities that were thrown up in the 60s and 70s. Architecture here is thoroughly eclectic. Gothic churches and Victorian warehouses punctuate the tower blocks, and cutting-edge architects have created dazzlingly original post-modern fusions such as the exceptional Public Library. Such exciting cityscapes have inspired a generation of film makers, making Vancouver's movie industry a serious competitor for Hollywood. Film people have brought their own level of hip to the city, the trendy *Alibi Room*, for instance, being owned and frequented by the likes of Gillian Anderson.

Working against such tendencies is a legacy of politicians and grey entities who instituted a set of draconian laws that denied liquor licences, limited opening hours and even outlawed dancing in certain places. This apparently deliberate ploy to stop people having too good a time led listings bible the *Georgia Strait* to dub Vancouver 'the city that fun forgot'. Though the laws have now changed, Vancouver has yet to become the happening spot it should be.

Like British Columbia as a whole, the scenic splendour of Vancouver's mountains and water is a perennial source of health and inspiration. This is the major outlet for BC's staggering number of artists and artisans, making it a great place to shop for art and crafts. BC is also renowned for its marijuana, resulting in Vancouver's dubious claim to be the new Amsterdam, with an as yet small number of 'smoke-friendly' cafés.

Halfway between Asia and Europe, Vancouver's character is less Canadian than it is Pacific Rim. Of all the world's cities, this is the one where East and West fuse most completely, a real-life example of the kind of futuristic multiculturalism that Ridley Scott foresaw in *Blade Runner*. Of five daily newspapers in Greater Vancouver, three are in Chinese; Chinese New Year is a far bigger occasion than 31 December; Chinese medicine clinics, schools and herbalists are ubiquitous. Vancouver's Chinatown is the continent's third biggest after New York and San Francisco, and Chinese food in Vancouver has been ranked equal to that of Hong Kong. But this is only one strand of a rich multicultural Oriental tapestry that also embraces immigrants from Hong Kong, Taiwan, the Philippines, Japan, South Korea, Malaysia and Singapore.

Unless you're coming from the United States or elsewhere in Canada, the only way to get to Vancouver is by air. There are frequent flights to Vancouver from London, Frankfurt and Amsterdam, and many cities in the US. Three weekly flights arrive from Australia and two from New Zealand. Flights from Europe are reasonably inexpensive, especially in the off-season. There are also frequent buses and trains from Seattle. Flights within Canada are relatively expensive.

Vancouver's Downtown is easily explored on foot. The fastest, most efficient form of local transport is the SkyTrain, but its destinations are limited. The local bus network is extensive, but services are slow, stop running around midnight, and tend to be confusing for visitors. The SeaBus makes the scenic journey to the North Shore, while useful private ferries ply the waters of False Creek. Taxis are affordable and numerous. Destinations further afield are reached by *Greyhound* buses and *BC Ferries*. Long waits for the latter are frequent in summer. Car rental is unnecessary except for longer excursions.

# Getting there

## Air

**From Europe** Only three airlines currently fly directly to Vancouver from the UK. **Air Canada** have14 flights per week and **British Airways** have seven flights per week, all from Heathrow. Often the best deals are with **Air Transat** who have four flights per week from Heathrow, one from Manchester and one from Glasgow (but no winter flights). There are no direct flights from Ireland. For passengers from mainland Europe, there are regular flights with **KLM**, **Lufthansa** and *Air Transat*. Whatever your starting point, the cheapest flights often involve changing planes in the United States. Booking far in advance or at the last minute are the other ways of lowering the price. Return flights from Europe average between £500 (or the equivalent in euro) in the low season and £750 in the high season. However, you can get them for as little as £350-400, and at peak times they may soar to over £1,000.

**From the United States** The major companies serving the US are **American Air**, **Continental Airlines**, **Northwest Airlines** and **United Airlines**. While booking ahead can save you money with an Apex fare, more often the best-value tickets are available at the last minute on the internet. The cheapest flights are in winter (apart from Christmas), with prices rising to their high-season rate around mid-April.

**Airport information** Vancouver International Airport (YVR), **T** 2077077, www.yvr.ca, is located on Sea Island at the mouth of the Fraser River, 13 km south of Downtown. The very modern International Terminal has all the usual facilities, including a BC Visitor Information desk on the Arrivals floor (level 2) and an Airport Information desk (with a lost and found service) one floor up in the Departure lounge, along with most of the shops and services. There are plenty of phones and ATMs, and the corridor

**Airlines and agents**

**Air Transat, T** 08705-561522 (UK), www.airtransat.com
**Air Canada, T** 08705-247226 (UK), www.aircanada.ca
**American Air, T** 1800-7337300 (US), www.aa.com
**British Airways, T** 08457-799977 (UK), www.british-airways.com
**Continental Airlines, T** 1800-2310856 (US), www.continental.com
**Delta Airlines, T** 1800-2414141 (US), www.delta-air.com
**KLM, T** 204-747747 (Amsterdam), www.klm.com
**Lufthansa, T** 01805-8384267 (Frankfurt), www.lufthansa.com
**Northwest Airlines, T** 1800-4474747 (US), www.nwa.com
**United Airlines, T** 1800-5382929 (US), www.ual.com

**Websites**
www.cheapflights.com; www.expedia.com
www.flynow.com; www.istc.org
www.statravel.com; www.travelocity.com

linking the international and domestic terminals has a children's play area and nursery.

All forms of transport heading Downtown are right outside the terminal. City bus No 100 is the cheapest ($3) but involves a transfer at 70th Avenue/Granville onto bus No 8, and takes a good hour. The *Airporter* shuttle bus, leaves every 15 minutes from 0630-0010, heading to the major Downtown hotels and Canada Place. Tickets ($12 one way, $18 return) can be bought at the Visitor Information desk, *Airporter* office, or on the bus itself. Taxis operate around the clock, charging $25-30 for the 25-minute trip Downtown. *Limojet Gold Express*, **T** 2731331, charge $40 for up to eight passengers. All the major car-rental agencies are located on the ground floor of the car park, across the road from Arrivals.

Vancouver airport is a safe and relaxed place. There is a hotel right in the airport and others are a short ride away in Richmond.

Almost all hotels have staff on duty 24 hours, or can cater for a late arrival if given due warning. If you're hungry or thirsty, head for *The Naam* or *Calhoun's* in Kitsilano, which stay open all night.

● *Before you leave the Arrivals building, go upstairs and see Bill Reid's sculpture,* Spirit of Haida Gwaii.

## Coach

The main route to Vancouver from the US is Highway 5 from Seattle, a three- to four-hour drive. The Peace Arch Border Crossing is extremely busy, especially at weekends, in summer and on Canadian or US holidays. It has a Visitor Information Centre, open daily. *Greyhound*, **T** 1800-2312222, www.greyhound.com, run six daily buses from Seattle to Vancouver, $22 ($40 return). *Quickshuttle*, **T** 9404428, www.quickshuttle.com, run eight daily services from Seattle to the Downtown *Holiday Inn* at 1110 Howe Street, $39 ($70 return), with reductions for students and children.

## Sea

Several American ferries run to Victoria: *MV Coho*, **T** 3862202, from Port Angeles, US$8 ($30 with vehicle); *Victoria Clipper*, **T** 3828100, from Seattle, US$75; and *Washington State Ferries*, **T** 3811551, from Anacortes (San Juan Island), US$11 ($29.75 with vehicle).

## Train

*Amtrak*, **T** 1800-8727245, www.amtrak.com, run one daily train from Seattle to Vancouver, leaving at 0745, arriving 1140. US$23-35 one-way, depending when you book.

# Getting around

## Air

An easy way to get to **Victoria** from Vancouver is with *Harbour Air Seaplanes*, **T** 5375525, www.harbour-air.com, who have regular flights from Canada Place to Victoria's Inner Harbour, $93 one-way.

**TransLink**

**Bus**, **SkyTrain** and **SeaBus** services are all operated by *TransLink*, **T** 5210400, www.translink.bc.ca  Tickets are valid on all three services for any number of journeys within a 90-minute period. The system is divided into three fare zones, with Zone One covering almost everything of interest. Fares are $2 for one zone, $3 for two zones and $4 for three zones. A day pass is $8, $6 for concessions. Information, including maps and timetables, is available at the Visitor Information Centre, public libraries, and SkyTrain ticket booths. *TransLink* also run **HandyDART**, **T** 4302892, a service for disabled travellers.

The quickest way to get to **Tofino** is by float-plane from the International Airport Seaplane Terminal, with *Atleo River Air Service*, **T** 7252205, atleoair@alberni.net,  $350 one-way, $550 return.

**Bus**
Vancouver's bus system is slow and often confusing for visitors. Exact fare is dropped into a machine which never gives change. If you have bought a ticket in the last 90 minutes (time of purchase on ticket), feed it into the machine, which will give it back.  Buses to most places can be caught Downtown from the pedestrianized section of Granville Street. For details of routes, see individual entries. Bus-stops and the vehicles themselves carry no information. Night buses stop running after about 0030.

To travel up the **Sea to Sky Highway** to **Whistler**, *Greyhound*, **T** 1800-6618747, www.greyhound.ca, run six daily buses (seven in winter) from Vancouver bus station. In winter their non-stop *Ski Express* leaves at 0630 arriving at Whistler at 0830. Alternatively, *Bigfoot's Snow Shuttle*, T7779905, runs to Whistler three times daily from all Vancouver hostels, $27 one way, $49 return. A combined *Airporter/Greyhound* ticket from the airport is $33 one-way.

*Perimeter Whistler Express*, **T** 2665386, picks up at the airport and major hotels and charges $55 ($43 concessions) one-way.

From Vancouver to **Victoria** is a short hop most easily made with *Pacific Coach Lines*, **T** 1800-6611725, www.pacificcoach.com, who operate at least 14 buses per day in summer, $29 adult, $20 concessions, $14.50 children, one-way including ferry.

**Tofino** can be reached by ferry from Horseshoe Bay to Nanaimo, then one of the two daily buses run by *Laidlaw Coach Lines*, **T** 1800-3180818, www.graylines.ca  The 0630 ferry will get you there in time for the 0840 bus, which stops at the ferry dock, and arrives in Tofino at 1250.

## Car

Driving in Vancouver is no more difficult than in any city, but narrow roads and a surfeit of vehicles make for slow-going and multiple traffic jams. It's less hassle to rely on public transport, but if you're planning an excursion, a vehicle can open up many possibilities. Petrol/gas is cheaper than in the UK but more expensive than in the US. The real problem is parking. Vacant meters are often hard to find and have two-hour limits, and the wardens are brutal. The best deals are in small open-air parking lots where you can pay for the whole day or evening. Seymour is a good place to start looking. Break-ins are fairly common, especially for vehicles with US plates, so park away from the sleazy East Side area, avoid back alleys, and leave nothing of value in your car. In areas like West Broadway, 4th Avenue and Commercial Drive, free available parking can often be found on adjacent streets such as 5th Avenue. All the major rental agencies have offices Downtown. See Directory, p225.

## Cycling

Measures have been taken to make the city less tough on cyclists. For a map of the ever-expanding network of bikeways and other useful information, see *Cycling in Vancouver*, available from the

## → Travel extras

Vancouver is an easy destination. There are no health risks or mandatory vaccinations, everything you could possibly need for your stay can be bought right here, probably cheaper than it would be at home, and money can be easily changed at any bank or bureau de change. It is advisable, however, to have health insurance, as visitors to Canada do not receive free treatment.

It must also be one of the world's safest cities. Even the sleazy East Side district along Hastings Street is more sad and troubling than actually dangerous. Having said that, any city has its hazards, so lone travellers, particularly women, should avoid dark, remote areas and back alleys at night. A small but conspicuous number of attacks have taken place on secluded trails in Stanley Park after dark in the last decade, so avoid such circumstances.

Tourist Information Centre or good bike stores. Many buses are equipped with bike racks, and bikes can be carried on ferries and the SeaBus. Bike lockers exist at most SkyTrain stations. Rental for a regular bike is about $15 per day, $70 per week. See Directory, p225.

### SeaBus and other ferries

The SeaBus, a passenger ferry that crosses Burrard Inlet between Waterfront SkyTrain Station and North Vancouver's Lonsdale Quay, leaves every 15 minutes and the crossing takes 12 minutes. The ferries are wheelchair accessible and can carry bikes. On False Creek, the *Aquabus* runs from the south end of Hornby Street to Science World, stopping at the Arts Club on Granville Island, the end of Davie Street in Yaletown, and behind Monk McQueens at Stamp's Landing. The fare for each stop is $2-3, depending on length of journey. *False Creek Ferries* run from the Maritime Museum in Vanier Park to Science World, stopping at the Aquatic

Centre on Beach Avenue, Granville Island Public Market, and Stamp's Landing. They charge $2-5 one way or $8 ($5 concessions) for a 40-minute tour.

For **Victoria**, BC Ferries, **T** 1888-7245223, www.bcferries.com, run from Vancouver's Tsawwassan, about 30 km south of Vancouver (bus No 404 and transfer to No 98 at Airport Junction, $4) and Swartz Bay, 40 km from Victoria at the north end of Saanich Peninsula (bus No 70 to Downtown, $2.50, or cycle the bike trail). Ferries leave every other hour, 0700-2100 or hourly at peak times, $9.50 single, $34 with vehicle, 95 minutes.

BC Ferries also run to the **Gulf Islands** from Tsawwassan and Swartz Bay. The schedules are very complex and subject to change, so pick up the latest timetable before making plans. Two ferries run per day from Vancouver to Galiano, a 50-minute journey; they continue to Mayne, Pender and Salt Spring (Long Harbour), should you want to do some island hopping. There are eight daily ferries between Salt Spring (Fulford Harbour) and Victoria, a 35-minute crossing. There are also four ferries from Victoria to Galiano and occasional direct crossings between Vancouver and Salt Spring. Gulf Island Water Taxi, **T** 5372510, connects Galiano and Salt Spring on Wednesday and Saturday in July and August, Saturday in June, $20 return, $5 per kayak.

From late May 2003 Harbour Lynx, T7534443, are to operate a passenger-only high-speed ferry from Vancouver's Waterfront SeaBus terminal to **Nanaimo**'s Inner Harbour. From there Tofino Bus Lines, T1866-9863466, run mini-buses to **Tofino**.

## SkyTrain

Vancouver's elevated light railway, the SkyTrain, is not only the fastest, most convenient way of getting from A to B, but it also provides an exciting way to see the city. However, there are only a few useful stops. Waterfront, in the old Canadian Pacific Railway Station next to Canada Place, is good for connecting with the SeaBus; Burrard at Burrard and Dunsmuir is the closest to the

Visitor Information Centre. Granville, beneath The Bay on Granville Street, is the best for Downtown and connections with buses. Science World-Main Street takes you right to the bus station. Broadway is good for Commercial Drive. SkyTrains run very frequently and ticket machines give change. First and last trains heading east from Waterfront are: Monday-Friday, 0508-0038; Saturday, 0608-0038; Sunday and holidays, 0708-2338.

### Walking

Walking is recommended anywhere within the Downtown Peninsula. From Chinatown to the Lion's Gate Bridge is unlikely to take more than an hour on foot, but distances outside the peninsula are usually too great to be undertaken on foot.

## Tours

### Walking tours

*Architectural Institute of BC*, 100-440 Cambie Street, **T** 6838588, www.aibc.bc.ca, run six different tours guided by architects that focus on each region's most interesting structures. These run Wednesday-Sunday, June-August. Areas covered are: Gastown, Chinatown, Downtown, West End, False Creek North and Yaletown and Strathcona (Vancouver's first residential area). All are free, last 1½-2 hours, and begin at 1330. Starting points are different for each tour, so phone or check their website for details. *Walkabout Historic Vancouver*, 6038 Imperial Street, **T** 7200006, www.darkroombytes.com/walkabout, run walking tours with costumed guides recounting stories and folklore.

### Bus tours

*Vancouver Trolley*, **T** 8015515, www.vancouvertrolley.com  These modern buses decked out to look like Vancouver's old trolley-buses run all round the Downtown Peninsula, Stanley Park, Vanier Park and Granville Island. There's no commentary, but if you're short of time, this is a good way to see most of what the city has to offer. Tours last two hours, but you can get on and off as many times as you wish. Buses leave from Gastown every 30 minutes, 0900-1430, $25 ($12 concessions) for a day ticket. *Vancouver Sightseeing Tours*, **T** 6855546, www.vancouversightseeingtours.com, run guided tours with commentary of Downtown, the North Shore or Whistler in a 10-person air-conditioned van. *The X-tour*, **T** 6092770, www.x-tour.com, run a variety of tours that take you round the sites used in filming the *X-files*, and other famous film and TV locations. Prices starts at $99, maximum seven people. For a few dollars more you can even spend the night in Scully's apartment.

## Boat tours

*Yellow Pages* are full of companies offering all kinds of luxurious boat tours around Vancouver. *False Creek Ferries* run cheap and cheerful tours from Granville Island, $8, $6 concessions, $4 children. *Champagne Cruises*, **T** 6888072, www.champagne cruises.com, at the other end of the scale, run a daily Sunset Dinner Cruise from 1730-2030 for $25. *Harbour Cruises*, north tip of Denman Street, **T** 6329697, www.boatcruises.com, operate all manner of tours, including Sunset Dinner Cruises, Indian Arm Luncheon Cruise and Vancouver Harbour Tour. *Sewell's Sea Safari*, 6695 Nelson Avenue, Horseshoe Bay, **T** 9213474, run 2½-hour Zodiac Tours for $55 ($25 concessions), with a good chance of spotting seals and eagles.

## Adventure tours around Vancouver

*Bigfoot Adventure Tours*, **T** 7779905, www.bigfoottours.com, run 2-10-day tours departing from hostels and aimed at young, independent travellers/backpackers. The 10-day 'Moose Run Tour' does a loop via Whistler, the Rockies and Kelowna, $380+tax. *EcoMountain Tours*, **T** 1800-9254453, www.ecomountaintours.com, can arrange anything from half-day to nine-day hiking tours with an emphasis on nature and aboriginal culture. Their five-day 'Coast

Mountain Traverse' takes you from the world's oldest Douglas fir forest in the Elaho Valley to hot springs in the Lillooet Valley ($750). *Explore BC Adventure Tours*, **T** 6891805, www.explore-bc.com, also offer a variety of tours including Grouse Mountain, nature walks, river-boat trips, rafting and flightseeing. *Lotus Land Tours*, **T** 6844922, www.lotuslandtours.com, run a broad range of activity-based tours in the Vancouver area, including eagle-watching, snow-shoeing, whale-watching, river-rafting, sea-kayaking and back-country hiking.

# Tourist information

The Visitor Information **Waterfront Centre**, 200 Burrard Street, is close to Canada Place at Plaza Level, **T** 6832000, www.tourism vancouver.com *Open daily mid-May to Sep 0800-1900, Oct to mid-May Mon-Fri 0830-1700, Sat 0900-1700.* They provide a full range of facilities including currency exchange, photo albums of hotels and B&Bs, a reservation service, tickets for events and excursions and full information about sights and transport. You can pick up the reasonably useful *Vancouver Book* and other free brochures for nearby destinations, such as *The Islands Vacation Guide*, which covers Vancouver Island, Victoria and the Gulf Islands or *Vancouver, Coast and Mountains*, which covers the Sea to Sky Highway. Sports enthusiasts should pick up the *Outdoor and Adventure Guide*, which will have them planning their next trip.

There is also a Tourist Information desk on the Arrivals floor (level 2) of **Vancouver International Airport**, **T** 3033603. *Open daily 0730-2330.* Another desk is at the **Peace Arch Border Crossing**. *Open daily 0800-2000 mid-Sep to mid-May and 0900-1700 mid-May to mid-Sep.* Should you need a map, *MapArt* publishing produce decent and cheap city maps, with full street index, in fold-out or book formats. They are widely available at gas stations, newsagents, book stores or souvenir outlets. *Rand McNally* also produce city maps and the best road atlas of British Columbia.

Vancouver

**Downtown and Yaletown  31**  Eclectic architecture, the Art Gallery, shops, bars and theatres and
the converted brick warehouses of trendy Yaletown.

**Gastown, East Side and Chinatown  40**  The first
quaint and touristy, the second sleazy and derelict,
the third rumbustious and stimulating.

**West End and Stanley Park  45**  A densely
populated neighbourhood, packed with restaurants
and cafés, next door to a vast, semi-wilderness park
with an Aquarium, seawall and giant trees.

**Granville Island and Vanier Park  49**  An
atmospheric maze of craft stores, galleries and
studios, a great Public Market and a waterfront park.

**Kitsilano and Point Grey  54**  Trendy neighbourhood and a string of sand beaches leading to the
university and exceptional Museum of Anthropology.

**South and East Vancouver  60**  A handful of
cosmopolitan, bohemian neighbourhoods and
delightful botanical gardens.

**North Shore  65**  A string of semi-wilderness parks
and canyons nestled in the mountain foothills.
Hiking, skiing, kayaking and mountain biking.

# Downtown and Yaletown

*Though tiny, Downtown Vancouver is the business and shopping hub of a sprawling suburban corridor that contains half the population of British Columbia, so naturally the atmosphere is quite intense. The **Art Gallery** and the small but top-notch **Canadian Craft and Design Museum** are both key sights, but the real reward comes in the shape of the richly varied architecture. Combined with frequent glimpses of snow-capped mountains and the pervasive oriental influence, Downtown Vancouver makes for fascinating strolling, but is best digested from the top of the **Lookout! Harbour Centre Tower**.*

▸▸ *See Sleeping p101, Eating and drinking p130, Bars and clubs p159*

## ◉ Sights

### Canada Place
*Map 3, C2, p252*

Canada Place juts out into the water of Burrard Inlet like a great ocean-going vessel, its five giant white 'masts' rising high above a powerful prow, begging obvious comparisons with Sydney's more famous Opera House. Built as the Canadian Pavilion for Expo '86, which celebrated the city's centenary, it now functions as a hotel, conference centre and the main terminus for Vancouver's raging cruise-ship business. Besides its scenic value, the only real interest for travellers is an **Imax theatre** inconveniently situated at the back. Across the road is the Visitor Information Centre.

### Marine Building
*355 Burrard St.  Map 3, C1, p252*

Designed to put Vancouver on the international shipping map, this strikingly magnificent construction was, and perhaps still is, the city's most notable building. Completed in 1930, it was the tallest building in the British Empire for over a decade, and was described by Sir John Betjeman as "the best art deco office building in the world". In keeping with the architect's vision of "some great crag rising from the sea", the relief frieze around its base and the brass surroundings of its double-revolving doors are dotted with an array of marine flora and fauna. The sumptuous façade is decorated with terracotta panels illustrating the discovery of the Pacific Ocean and the history of transport, including zeppelins, trains and some famous ships like the *Golden Hind* and the *Resolution*. Over the main entrance, Captain Vancouver's ship the *Discovery* is seen on the horizon, with Canada geese flying across the stylized sunrays. The sumptuous lobby, designed to resemble a Mayan temple, is well worth a look too.

## Lookout! Harbour Centre Tower

555 W Hastings St, **T** 2999000, www.vancouverlookout.com
*Daily 0830-2130 summer, 0900-2100 winter. $9, $6 concessions for 1-day multiple entries, including guided tour. Map 3, D3, p252*

Distinctive with its flying saucer-shaped top level, the Harbour Centre Tower is no longer the tallest building in BC, but the Lookout! observation deck still gives the best close-up 360° views of the city, particularly striking at sunset on a clear day. Glass-walled elevators on the outside of the building whisk you up 167 m in 50 seconds, and though the ticket is expensive, it allows as many returns on the same day as you wish. Every hour, guides recount the history of the many sights you can see from here.

● *A short stroll east at 848 W Hastings is the **Pacific Mineral Museum** (see Museums, p74), whose large collection includes meteorites, all kinds of fossils and a treasure chest of gems and semi-precious stones. The gift shop sells more of the same.*

## Canadian Pacific Railway Station (CPR)

601 W Cordova St. *Map 3, C2, p252*

Almost opposite at 601 West Cordova Street is the old Canadian Pacific Railway Station. Built in 1914, this neoclassical beaux-arts-style building with its arches and white-columned façade is now the eastern terminus of the SkyTrain, and behind it is the *SeaBus* terminal. Major restoration in 1978 thankfully retained many features of the original magnificent interior such as the high ceilings, delicate woodworking and tile floor.

## Vancouver Art Gallery

750 Hornby St, **T** 6624700, www.vanartgallery.bc.ca  *Jun-Sep Fri-Wed 1000-1730, Thu 1000-1900, Oct-May closed Mon. $12.50, $9 seniors, $8 students, free for children under 12; suggested donation of $5 on Thu evenings.  Map 2, E8, p250*

Vancouver's original courthouse, an imposing neoclassical marble building, was designed in 1910 by Francis Rattenbury (see p237), the architect responsible for Victoria's Legislative Building and *Empress Hotel*. In 1983 it was renovated by Arthur Erickson (see p238) and today its four spacious floors house the largest art gallery in Western Canada. Of the 7,000 works in its collection, only the Emily Carr Gallery is a permanent fixture, but this justifies a visit in itself. The world's largest collection of works by this prominent Victoria artist (see p237) are rotated and accompanied by a video on her life and art. Otherwise there are temporary exhibitions, usually  contemporary. There are Curator's Tours on Sundays at 1400; discussions in the *Philosophers' Café* on Thursdays at 1900; occasional symposiums; and the Open Studio, where visitors and their kids are given material to create their own related pieces of art. There are also art courses and occasional concerts. The gallery shop is a great place for original crafts. The catacombs are said to house a ghost named Charlie, believed to be the spirit of William Charles Hopkinson, an immigration officer murdered there in 1914.

● *To the west of the Art Gallery is one of the city's most distinctive landmarks, the* **Hotel Vancouver**. *A typical example of the grand*

**Lookout!**
*The best overall view of Downtown Vancouver is from the top of the Harbour Centre Tower, once the city's tallest building.*

★ **Viewpoints**

**Best**
- Grouse Mountain, p69
- Patio of the Rusty Gull, p167
- Seasons in the Park, p143
- Behind the Museum of Anthropology, p56
- Mount Gardner, Bowen Island, p64

*hotels erected across Canada by the Canadian Pacific Railway, this hulking Gothic castle sports a striking green copper roof, gargoyles and some fine relief sculpture. It's worth wandering in to admire the opulent interior.*

### Christ Church Cathedral
*Map 2, D8, p250*

Opposite the *Hotel Vancouver*, and all the more distinctive for its location amidst such towering edifices, is Vancouver's oldest surviving church, Christ Church Cathedral, completed in 1895. The Gothic Revival style of this buttressed sandstone building is reminiscent of English parish churches, with a steep gabled roof, and some impressive pointed-arch stained-glass windows. Inside, the timber framework is also splendid.

### Canadian Craft and Design Museum
639 Hornby St, **T** 6878266. *Mon-Sat 1000-1700, Sun 1200-1700, Thu 1000-2100. Closed Tue, Sep-May. $5, $3 concessions, by donation Thu after 1700. Map 3, D1, p252*

Nextdoor to the Cathedral, Cathedral Place is a marvellous staggered glass-and-granite edifice with fine details etched into its rock and a roof that clearly pays homage to the facing hotel. A neo-Gothic lobby packed with art deco details leads to a lovely grassed courtyard and the small, but extremely worthwhile, Canadian Craft and Design Museum. Innovative exhibits highlight the artesan expertise for which BC is so highly reputed, with works in a variety of media including clay, glass, wood, metal and fibre.

● *Next door is the sleek **HSBC Building** whose towering atrium lobby contains the world's largest pendulum and one of Vancouver's best unofficial art galleries. It's also a relaxing place to stop for a coffee.*

## Robson Square and around
*Map 2, E8, p250*

While renovating the old courthouse, Erickson designed the new Provincial Law Courts two blocks south on Hornby and Smithe. A steel-framed mass of sloping glass roofs and walls, it represents a radical departure from the tendency of courts to be closed off and intimidating. This one is so accessible you can literally walk on it. The building is part of the larger complex of Robson Square, whose landscaped public space is a favourite summer gathering spot.

## Vancouver Public Library
350 W Georgia St, *T* 3313600, www.vpl.vancouver.bc.ca  *Mon-Thu 1000-2000, Fri-Sat 1000-1700, Sun 1300-1700.  Map 3, F2, p252*

Four blocks west from the Art Gallery is the remarkable Vancouver Public Library. Despite architect Moshe Safdie's denials, its circular walls and tiered arches do bear an uncanny resemblance to the Roman Colosseum. This post-modern masterpiece appears strangely ancient and futuristic at the same time. As well as the seven-level library, a square within a circle, the complex includes a 21-storey government building, and a pleasant shop-filled atrium spanned by a couple of elegant bridges.

**!**
**●** Vancouver Public Library was spectacularly blown up at the end of the Arnold Schwarzenegger film *The Sixth Day*.

## Cathedral of Our Lady of the Rosary
646 Richards St. *Map 3, E2, p252*

Two blocks from the library, this is a handsome Gothic Revival structure from the late 1880s. Key features include asymmetrical towers, the pointed arches of windows and doorways, a vaulted ceiling and an octave of eight bells that are still rung by hand each Sunday. The oldest of the stained-glass windows is found in the Lady Chapel to the left of the altar.

## Yaletown
*Map 2, H8, p251 and Map 3, G1, p253*

Situated south of the Downtown in a small triangle of land hemmed in by Pacific Boulevard, Homer and Nelson, Yaletown was once the rowdy warehouse district, with more saloons per hectare than anywhere else in the world. Recently, the massive old brick buildings have inspired a renaissance, with architects and entrepreneurs falling over themselves to develop the kind of spacious apartments and trendy bars and restaurants that the young and upwardly mobile love to frequent. Many of the establishments walk a thin line between panache and pretentiousness, and the whole zone needs time to mellow into a genuine sense of style. Still, it is a fascinating area which is at its best at night, when the many fine eating and watering holes come to life.

## BC Place Stadium
Robson St/Beatty, **T** 6875520 *Daily 1000-1700. $6, $4 concessions for museum. Stadium SkyTrain station; False Creek Ferry; Bus No 2, 15 or 17 on Burrard or No 5 on Granville. Map 3, H2, p253*

The world's largest air-supported dome when it opened in 1983, BC Place is known to Vancouverites as the 'Marshmallow in Bondage'. As well as a 60,000-seat venue for the city's major sports

### Gassy Jack

One of Vancouver's favourite historic characters is the garrulous Yorkshireman 'Gassy' Jack Deighton. He first appeared on the scene running a bar in New Westminster that profited from the Caribou Gold Rush traffic of 1862. But history remembers him best rowing across Burrard Inlet with his native wife, her mother and cousin, a yellow dog, two chairs and a barrel of whisky. Knowing that the nearest drink was a 5-km row then 15-km walk away, he offered a bunch of thirsty workers at Stamp's Mill all the whisky they could drink if they helped him build a bar. Within 24 hours the *Globe Saloon* was finished, and soon became the focus of the area that came to be known as Gastown.

teams, it contains the BC Sports Hall of Fame and Museum, with hands-on displays highlighting the lives and achievements of the province's top athletes.

● *Outside is the* **Terry Fox Memorial**, *a tribute to the local hero who died in 1981 attempting to run the width of Canada to raise money for cancer research. It's a strange and unpopular brick, tile and steel structure intended to recall a Roman triumphal arch.*

### Science World

1455 Quebec St, **T** 4437440, www.science world.bc.ca *1000-1700 Mon-Fri, 1000-1800 weekends. $12.75, $8.50 concessions; $17.75, $13.50 concessions with Omnimax; $13.50, $10.50 concessions for Omnimax double bill. SkyTrain; False Creek Ferry; Bus No 3 or 8 on Granville or Hastings, No 19 on Pender, all 3 on Main. Map 3, I5, p253 See also p221*

Another of Vancouver's notable structures is the giant geodesic dome that makes a suitably futuristic venue for Science World. Best appreciated from the SkyTrain, this silver golf ball is lit up at night with thousands of lights. Outside is a massive moving sculpture that rattles and rings. Don't be put off by the lightweight ground floor; almost all of the interesting stuff is in the Main Gallery on Level 2. A wealth of interactive, mind-bending and thoroughly educational exhibits will keep anyone, not just kids, entertained for at least a couple of hours. The Kidspace Gallery has lots of hands-on stuff for younger children, while the Sara Stern Search Gallery does a good job of making environmental lessons fun. The Alcan Omnimax theatre upstairs has the edge over even the giant Imaxes by showing films on a huge dome screen with wrap-around visuals and sound. Shows last 40 minutes.

# Gastown, East Side and Chinatown

*Gastown, Vancouver's oldest quarter, was the original site of the city's first industry and the famous saloon of 'Gassy' Jack Deighton, after whom the district was named. Extensive renovations during the 1960s were designed to convert the run-down, neglected remains of this historic district into a tourist haven. There are some handsome old buildings that are perfect venues for* **bars and restaurants**, *and the cobblestoned streets lead off to hidden alcoves and mews that are undeniably quaint. A string of tacky* **souvenir stores** *and the area's over-hyped* **Steam Clock** *sadly pander to the tour-bus brigade, yet the area is also incongruously emerging as the city's hotspot for* **nightclubs** *and contains the greatest concentration of antique/curiosity stores, retro clothes boutiques, commercial art galleries and purveyors of quality First Nations crafts.*

*In a strange tug-of-war, Vancouver's seediest quarter,* **East Side**, *lies immediately adjacent to the overtly touristy Gastown. Over a century ago, when the city's first streetcars connected Gastown to a newly emerging business district along Granville, Hastings Street entered a decline that has led to its current rating as Canada's lowest-income postal district. Despite several attempts to clean up the area,* *the blocks east of Cambie are lined with derelict buildings and closed shops, peopled by bums, addicts, drug-dealers and prostitutes.*

*True to Vancouver's predominantly Pacific Rim persona, the streets of **Chinatown** are lined with noisy shops selling the kind of weird and wonderful ingredients only the Chinese would know how to cook: unusual fruits, tanks full of obscure shellfish, dubious parts of a pig's anatomy, huge barrels full of tiny dried fish or shrimp. The main sight is the **Dr Sun Yat-Sen Classical Chinese Garden**, the first authentic Ming Classical garden built since 1492, and the first ever outside China.*

▸▸ *See Sleeping p104, Eating and drinking p134, Bars and clubs p162, Gay and lesbian p213 and Shopping p191*

# ◉ Sights

### Gastown
*Map 3, D3, p252*

The heart of Gastown is **Water Street** which contains the much-touted **Steam Clock**. In 1977 clockmaker Ray Saunders decided that the underground steam pipes that heat local buildings could also be used to power a clock, and constructed one to prove it. At 5 m tall, this is not as imposing as one expects, though its four-sided glass face, 20-kg gold-plated pendulum and Gothic-style roof are attractive enough. Every 15 minutes it entertains tourists by tooting and erupting in a cloud of steam.

Further east at the junction of Water, Powell and Alexander streets is the charming **Maple Leaf Square**. A statue of Gassy Jack standing on a whisky barrel is a work of imagination on the part of sculptor Vern Simpson, as no-one knows what the Yorkshireman

Chinatown is said to be riddled with mysterious underground tunnels. A city work crew accidentally stumbled on one when doing repairs on Alexander Street, and they simply filled it in.

### East meets West

Chinese immigrants have played an important role throughout Vancouver's history, but they have not always been made so welcome. The first Chinese settlers arrived in 1858, coming up from San Francisco during the Fraser Valley Gold Rush. In 1875 Queen Victoria gave assent to an act passed in the BC legislature to deny the vote to Chinese and Native people, a law that remained in effect for more than 70 years. During the 1880s, a great influx helped to build the BC section of the CPR, receiving half the wage of their white fellows, and often used as cannon fodder during dynamite blasting. Estimates are that three Chinese lives were lost for every kilometre of track laid in the almost impenetrable Fraser Canyon. Open public hostility against the so-called 'Yellow Peril' included rallies, campaigns and rampaging mobs. Over 24 items of anti-Chinese legislation were passed in BC from 1878-1913 alone, including head-taxes that gradually rose to $500 in 1903. A century later things have changed somewhat, and more subtle arrangements exist whereby many newcomers are admitted under the Immigrant Investor Program, meaning their money is put into real estate, hotels and restaurants, manufacturing and media.

looked like beyond a description of his complexion being 'muddy purple'. Opposite is the thin curved end of the wedge-shaped **Hotel Europe** (1909), the first reinforced-concrete building in Vancouver and certainly one of its most attractive constructions. Behind Gassy Jack is the site of his second saloon after the 1886 fire. Made from Chinese bricks used as ballast in sailing vessels, the **Byrne's Block** is Vancouver's oldest brick building. Secreted behind it is **Gaoler's Mews**, an atmospheric little courtyard full of trees, old-fashioned lampposts, park benches and a sundial.

## East Side

*Map 3, E6, p252*

The corner of Hastings and Main has become notorious as the focal point for the sad and sleazy underworld. The recent grizzly multiple murder of women from the East Side has once again shone the media's spotlight on this notorious quarter, which mayor Larry Campbell (see p236) has vowed to clean up. Nevertheless, this strangely compelling district is safe enough to wander through even at night, and contains some of the last remaining examples of neon in Vancouver. It's also the focus of a few 'smoke-friendly' cafés that are touting Vancouver as the New Amsterdam, and contains some interesting and wonderfully eclectic buildings. The 19th-century French Classical-style **Dominion Building** at 207 West Hastings is one of the city's most attractive pieces of architecture, with an elaborately decorated red-brick and yellow terracotta veneer and a distinctive beaux-arts-style roof. In 1910 this, the British Empire's highest structure, stood opposite Vancouver's public focus, Victory Square, now run-down and nicknamed 'Pigeon Park'. Two years later its record height was topped by the nearby **Sun Tower** at 100 West Pender. As a publicity stunt in 1920, Houdini suspended himself from its green copper roof.

● *Just east of Main at 280 Cordova is the* **Firehall Arts Centre**, *and at No 303 is* **St James Anglican Church**, *a fine structure that combines touches of the Romanesque, Gothic, Byzantine and modern.*

## ★ Chinatown

*Map 3, F6, p252*

The **Dr Sun Yat-Sen Classical Chinese Garden**, 578 Carrall Street, **T** 6897133, *$7.50, $5 concessions*, Chinatown's star attraction, is an authentic Ming Classical garden created by 52 experts flown in, along with most of the raw materials, from Suzhou, China's 'City of Gardens'. It is a carefully planned world of symmetry and balance, simplicity and symbolism. There are walls within walls, courtyards within courtyards, pavilions, halls, bridges and covered galleries. Guided tours, included in the admission fee, are essential for an understanding of the Taoist rinciples at work.

The **Chinese Cultural Centre**, 555 Columbia Street, **T** 6588865, www.cccvan.com, *Tue-Sun 1100 to 1700. $3, $2 concessions*, an ugly concrete building with a colourful gate, is very much geared towards the local Chinese community rather than tourists, but it does contain a museum with some interesting artefacts and information for those who want to know more about the history of Vancouver's Chinese community (see box, p42). The permanent exhibition *From Generation to Generation* tells the story of Canadian Chinese from the Gold Rush to the present. There are also temporary exhibits, and a collection dedicated to the Chinese Canadian Military.

Tours of Chinatown, *daily Jun-Sep 1000-1400, $10, $8 senior, $2.50 child*, make much of the novel **Sam Kee Building** at 8 West Pender. Legend has it that when the fledgling city appropriated most of Chang Toy's 9-m lot for street widening, his neighbour expected to get the remaining 1.8 m at a bargain price. To frustrate him, Toy constructed the world's skinniest building and put a popular bath-house in the basement. Known as 'Slender on Pender', it is 1.8 m wide, 30 m long and two storeys high. More intriguing is the widely substantiated rumour that the whole of Chinatown is riddled with secret underground tunnels. Ask the tour guide for their angle on this mystery.

The sights and smells of Chinatown are at their most intense in the open-air **Night Market**, 200 Keefer Street, *summer Fri-Sun 1830-2300*. Consider eating here too, the restaurants are as good as you'll ever find outside China; at the very least try a curried beef bun from one of the bakeries.

# West End and Stanley Park

*Downtown Vancouver is immediately adjacent to Canada's most densely populated district, which also houses the largest gay community west of Toronto. The **West End** is roughly contained by Thurlow, Robson, Denman and Davie streets, the last three of which represent the focal points of a young and lively neighbourhood. The best streets for walking west to Stanley Park are **Robson** and **Davie**. The former starts off as Vancouver's main shopping drag, the place to buy and then show off the latest hip designer wear, then is taken over by hotels and restaurants. The latter, like **Denman**, possesses a much more typical West End neighbourhood atmosphere. Their cafés and restaurants perpetually buzzing, these are prime streets for menu-browsing. **Sunset Beach** on English Bay is the one favoured by locals.*

*▸▸ See Sleeping p105, Eating and drinking p135, Bars and clubs p164, Gay and lesbian p213*

##  Sights

### Roedde House Museum

1415 Barclay St, **T** 6847040, www.roeddehouse.org   *Admission by guided tour only. Phone to arrange. $5, $3 concessions. Bus No 5 to Broughton.   Map 2, C5, p250*

Sadly, most of the West End's traditional buildings were replaced during the development boom of the 1960s with over 200 high-rises. The best surviving block is **Barclay Heritage Square**, whose park-like setting contains nine historic houses built between 1890 and 1908. One 1893 home, built for GA Roedde, Vancouver's first bookbinder, is furnished in Edwardian style and has been converted into Roedde House Museum, the West End's only real 'sight'.

**!** Bill Clinton once jogged the loop round Stanley Park with a posse of 30 black-suited bodyguards in tow.

## Stanley Park

T 2578400, www.parks.vancouver.bc.ca   *The main access roads are: Georgia St/Stanley Park Causeway to the east, Robson St in the centre, and Davie St/Beach Av to the west. Bus No 135 daytime Mon-Sat, No 23 or 25 evening/Sun/ holidays. Vehicle traffic is one-way and anti-clockwise. Parking anywhere in the park is $1/2 hrs or $3 for all day. A free shuttle bus runs right round the park every 15 mins from Jun-mid-Sep.   Map 4*

The bulk of this 400-ha evergreen oasis, Canada's biggest urban park, has been allowed to remain largely undeveloped. Many of the lonely trails (best avoided after dark) that lead through giant cedar, hemlock and fir were once skid roads used by loggers to drag massive trees to the water with teams of oxen. An obvious highlight is the stump of one such giant, now known as the **Hollow Tree**. Near here, on the path towards Third Beach is a living cedar – almost 5 m in diameter and roughly 1,000 years old – believed by *National Geographic* to be one of the world's largest trees and oldest cedars.

   To protect this semi-wilderness core from overuse, most of the park's infrastructure and attractions are concentrated on a peninsula, jutting eastwards resembling a duck's bill. Entering from Georgia Street, you'll pass the **Lost Lagoon**, a haven for many birds including swans, geese and the odd blue heron. The **Nature House**, *0900-1900 except Tue*, on its south shore offers ecological information and very useful maps. The *Ecology Society*, T 2578544, www.stanleyparkecology.ca, organizes Sunday Discovery Walks ($5), birding and various other free/cheap activities mainly for kids.

   Due east is the sheltered **Coal Harbour**. Next to *Vancouver Rowing Club* is an information booth and base of the one-hour horse-drawn tours that run round the park every 20-30 minutes, *mid-May-Oct, $14.95, $9.95 concessions*. To the north is a formal Rose Garden and the open-air Malkin Bowl, home in July and August to *Theatre Under the Stars*, see Festivals p186. Further on is a handful of attractions for kids and a Water Park.

The best thing about downtown Vancouver is that you can catch a glimpse of freedom at the end of the street.

*Al Fotheringham, comedian*

To the east on Avison Way is the Aquarium (see p48) and main car park.

Further round Coal Harbour is **Deadman's Island**, where the Coast Salish buried their dead. On **Brockton Point** is a decent stand of Kwakiutl and Haida totem poles, a picturesque old light-house and a number of monuments celebrating characters like Queen Victoria and David Oppenheimer, and the lovely *Girl in a Wetsuit*. At the spit's eastern point is the 9 O'Clock Gun, a cannon fired each evening at that hour. The tradition that began a century ago to signal the end of the day's legal fishing has continued almost unbroken ever since.

In summer, locals flock to the 9-km seawall which runs round the park's perimeter offering sea and mountain views. It's a first-class walk, jog, roller-blade or bike ride. Equipment can be hired from numerous stores at the north end of Denman Street. Cyclists and roller-bladers begin the circuit here, moving in an anti-clockwise direction.

On a hot day though, you'll want to join locals at the beaches and attractions around English Bay on the park's west side. Surrounding the *Fish House Restaurant* are tennis courts, lawn bowling and an 18-hole pitch and putt golf course (*$9.25, $7 concessions*). Nearby is a **Rhododendron Garden** featuring many other ornamental trees, including azaleas, camellias and several species of magnolia. **Second Beach** is just north, with a heated oceanside swimming pool. Further round the seawall are **Third Beach**, the *Teahouse Restaurant* and several viewpoints, of which Prospect Point at the northern, most elevated, tip is the best.

### ★ Vancouver Aquarium Marine Science Centre

Avison Way, **T** 6593474, www.vanaqua.org *Daily 1000-1730, in summer 0930-1900. $14.95, $11.95 concessions, $8.95 children, under 3s free. Bus No 135 from Hastings. There's also a free shuttle bus around the park in summer. Map 4, D6, p254*

One of Vancouver's prime rainy-day activities, the Aquarium is even better when the sun shines, as most of the exciting animals are outside. Entertaining as they may be, the seals, dolphins and otters are all utterly upstaged by a pair of giant and graceful white beluga whales. These extraordinary beings are best admired from the vantage of the underwater viewing room down-stairs, where a wealth of background information includes a video of the female giving birth. The whales are best saved till last though, as the other 20,000 creatures from the world's many seas tend to pale by comparison. Indoor highlights include the Treasures of the BC Coast gallery, with a giant Pacific octopus, coral, anemones and some eerily beautiful jellyfish. Next door is a large collection of handsome frogs. The Tropical and Amazon galleries are worth exploring: as well as colourful fish there are caymans, anaconda, lizards, snakes and even birds. Before even entering the Aquarium, look out for Bill Reid's magnificent bronze sculpture of a killer whale, *The Chief of the Undersea World* (1984).

# Granville Island and Vanier Park

*When Vancouver was first founded, False Creek was five times the size it is today. Land has been reclaimed all around the water, much of it for Expo '86. Originally no more than a sand bar, the area now known as Granville Island had been built up into an unsightly industrial zone when, in 1973, this ugly duckling was transformed into the most attractive shopping and arts district in the city. The atmosphere here, neither tacky nor rampantly commercial, compares to London's Covent Garden, except in the more conducive setting of water and boats. Besides the anomalous cement factory – a bizarre throwback to less picturesque days – this is the domain of yachting repair shops and charter companies, restaurants and cafés, theatres and buskers, the food and Kids' markets, and most notably Vancouver's artist and artisan community. Though not strictly pedestrianized, the island is well geared to aimless strolling.*

*East from Granville Island, a pleasant seawall path along False Creek connects a series of parks, marinas and small communities such as Stamp's Landing, a fine spot for a drink or meal. To the west of the island and Burrard Bridge, where False Creek widens into English Bay, another footpath leads to the 12-ha Vanier Park. As well as a popular summer hang-out and festival venue, with ponds, trees and plenty of lawn and beach, this park also contains the* **Vancouver Museum**, **HR MacMillan Space Centre** *and the* **Maritime Museum**.

▸▸ *See Sleeping p108, Eating and drinking p139, Bars and clubs p164*

#  Sights

### ★ Granville Island

*Most places are closed on Mon. South of Downtown across False Creek. Take the Aquabus, False Creek Ferry or Bus No 50 from Granville St and walk. Map 2, J4, p251*

If you arrive by bus, you'll find the **Kids' Market** hard to miss. Full of retail stores catering exclusively to the wee ones, this is an obvious stop for families. It's also a good place to start, as a couple of buildings away is the **Visitor Information Centre**, *T* 6665784, *0900-1800*, which provides a *Visitors' Guide* that includes a very useful map, and discount vouchers for many establishments. Behind here, the **Waterpark**, *May-Sep*, is an aquatic play area for kids, with multiple slides and a playground.

If you arrive by ferry, it will drop you right outside the wonderful **Public Market**. The building itself is a fine lesson in the renovation of industrial structures, making great use of the natural lighting, large windows and doors, heavy timber and steel. As well as a mouthwatering collection of international fast food stalls, the place is packed with every kind of fresh, innovative and tempting produce imaginable, from gourmet breads to seafood to sausages. The courtyard outside and adjacent bars are good places to watch the aquatic world float by. Nearby, **Granville Island Brewing Co**,

**Vanier Park**
*This popular summer hang-out and festival venue is also home to two museums and the HR MacMillan Space Centre.*

Canada's first microbrewery, runs 40-minute tours daily at 1200, 1400 and 1600, $8.75, $2.50 concessions, including a decent round of tasters and a souvenir glass. Their taproom is open Tuesday-Sunday 1200-1800, serving tapas-style dishes. Many fine arts shops are grouped together in the **Net Loft** and along **Railspur Alley**.

## Sport Fishing, Model Ships and Model Trains Museums

1502 Duranleau St, **T** 6831939, www.sportfishingmuseum.ca, www.modelshipsmuseum.ca, www.modeltrainsmuseum.ca *1000-1730. $6.50, $5 seniors, $3.50 children. Map 2, J4, p215   See also p222*

Tucked away in the **Maritime Market** these three museums rolled into one represent one of Vancouver's most unexpected delights. Even if you have just a passing interest in fishing or models, go! The collections are vast, world-class and lovingly displayed. The Sport Fishing Museum boasts the world's largest displayed collections of Hardy reels and hand-tied fly plates, as well as a fine array of split-cane fly rods and many other notable pieces. The world's largest collection of model and toy trains lives upstairs, topped off by a fabulous O-scale working layout that took six people 20,000 hours to complete. For most visitors, however, the highlight will be the extensive collection of model ships and submarines, with several dozen huge pieces that are all one-offs and demonstrate an obsessive and loving attention to detail.

## HR MacMillan Space Centre and Vancouver Museum

1100 Chestnut St, Vanier Park, **T** 7387827, www.hrmacmillan spacecentre.com   *1000-1700, closed Mon Sep-Jun. $12.75, $9.75 concessions, $8.75 children, under 5s free.* Vancouver Museum, **T** 7364431, www.vanmuseum.bc.ca   *1000-1700, Thu 1000-2100. Closed Mon in winter. $10, $8 seniors, $6 children, under 4s free. With Space Centre $17, $11 children. Bus No 2 or 22 from Burrard, then walk, or ferry from the Aquatic Centre.   Map 2, H2, p251   See also p222*

Housed in an interesting building whose shape resembles a circus big-top, but was actually inspired by the hats of Haida natives, is the upbeat HR MacMillan Space Centre. Outside is a funky metal fountain in the shape of a crab. Inside, a collection of interactive exhibits in the *Cosmic Courtyard* aims to introduce kids to such weighty topics as the Earth's geological composition, the nature of life in space and the logistics of space travel. The Planetarium has a rather dated feel that adds greatly to its appeal and has been very popular since the 1970s. It hosts a variety of 40-minute shows hourly in the afternoon. On Thursday to Saturday evenings are special laser shows set to the music of bands like Radiohead or Pink Floyd, *$9-11*. The Ground Station Canada Theatre hosts 20-minute shows that are basically video-assisted lectures involving a few wacky experiments designed to keep the kids interested. Tickets include as many of these and the Planetarium shows as desired, plus one 15-minute ride in the Virtual Voyages Simulator. There is also a free Observatory for star-gazing.

In the same building as the Space Centre, and devoted exclusively to the short career of this city, the Vancouver Museum could easily bore those with no special interest in that history. A small collection of artefacts and recreated scenes tells the story of the first explorers and settlers. Usually of greater interest are the temporary exhibits that home in on more unusual aspects of the region's past.

---

## Maritime Museum

1905 Ogden Av, Vanier Park, **T** 2578300, www.vmm.bc.ca  *Tue-Sat 1000-1700,  Sun 1200-1700. $8, $5.50 concessions, under 5s free. Bus No 2 or 22 from Burrard, then walk, or ferry from the Aquatic Centre.  Map 2, G1, p251*

---

A short walk west from the Vancouver Museum, this is a real treat for fans of sea-faring vessels. The first thing you see upon entering is the *RCMP St Roch*, which rightly holds pride of place, for it is an extraordinary vessel. A video on its history recounts all the firsts achieved by this hardy little schooner: first to travel the treacherous and long-sought Northwest Passage, a 27-month journey from Vancouver to Halifax; first to make the same journey back via the faster, more northerly route; first to circumnavigate North America. This front part of the museum, with its distinctive steep triangular shape, was actually built around the ship, which was lovingly restored to its 1944 condition and can now be explored. The museum contains plenty of other artefacts and stories, a fun exhibit on pirates, a hands-on area for kids and some bigger remnants scattered over the lawn outside. There is usually an interesting guest exhibit too.

In the west of the park, at 1150 Chestnut Street, is the **City of Vancouver Archives**, **T** 7368561, *0930-1730 Mon-Fri*, a vast and wonderful collection of old photos, books, maps and clippings.

# Kitsilano and Point Grey

*Vanier Park blends seamlessly into **Kits Beach**, one of the trendiest and most popular stretches of sand in the city, with great views of English Bay, Downtown and the Coast Mountains. A short stroll further on, Kitsilano is one of the most interesting neighbourhoods in the city. From here, Fourth Avenue and the more scenic Point Grey Road lead west to the jutting nose of Point Grey, passing **Hastings Mill Store**, Vancouver's oldest building, and some of the city's best sand beaches, on their way to the University of British Columbia (UBC). It's a long journey that is amply rewarded by the unmissable **Museum of Anthropology**. Nearby is the extensive **UBC Botanical Garden** and the serene **Nitobe Memorial Garden**. The peninsula also contains the extensive wide-open grounds of **Pacific Spirit Regional Park**, and a lovely trail runs all round the coast, passing through **Wreck Beach**, Vancouver's official, very popular nude beach.*

❯❯ *See Sleeping p108, Eating and drinking p140, Bars and clubs p165*

# ⊙ Sights

## Kitsilano

*Bus No 2 or 22 south on Burrard to Cornwall then walk to beach;
4th Av/Kitsilano: Bus No 4 or 7; West Broadway: Bus No 10 or 16.
Map 5, p255*

In the 1960s Kitsilano was the main focus of Vancouver's sub-
culture, the city's answer to Haight Ashbury in San Francisco. By
the 80s, many of those hippies had secured high-paying jobs,
bought and restored their houses and helped turn Kits into
Yuppie-ville. Reflecting this change, many of the old wooden
town houses that used to grace the area have been torn down
and replaced by condos. A lot of genuine character remains,
however, with an atmosphere somewhere between alternative
and affluent. The region's most interesting strips, **West 4th
Avenue** between Burrard and Macdonald, and **West Broadway**
(9th Avenue) between Macdonald and Alma, are well worth
exploring, containing many of the city's best speciality stores
and restaurants. Weekend brunch here is a Vancouver institution.
   **Kitsilano Outdoor Pool**, **T** 7310011, *May 22-Sep 12, 1200-
2045, from 1000 weekends, $4, $2.50 seniors, $1 children*, is the
biggest and most popular in Vancouver. The adjacent **Kitsilano
Showboat** is an outdoor theatre for summer productions.

## Kitsilano to UBC

*For Jericho Beach, bus No 4 or 44; for Spanish Banks, Locarno and
Wreck beaches, No 4, 7 or 44 to Alma, then No 42. Map 1, G1-G3, p249*

A wonderful trail runs right round the perimeter of Point Grey,
linking an almost uninterrupted string of beaches. First of these is
**Jericho Beach**, set in a large, very scenic park with a fine *Youth
Hostel*, an art gallery/theatre, a sailing school and a bird sanctuary.

Three unbroken kilometres connect it to **Locarno Beach**, a quiet area popular with families, and **Spanish Banks**, which has a beach café and warm, shallow water ideal for paddling. Beyond the museum (see below), roughly where Marine Drive meets University Blvd, about 100 steps lead down through the forest to the 6-km strip of **Wreck Beach**. On a hot day as many as 10,000 sun-worshippers take advantage of its clothing optional status, while wandering peddlars supply them with cold beers and food. Much of Point Grey's interior is occupied by **Pacific Spirit Regional Park**, also known as the Endowment Lands, 35 sq km of wild forest criss-crossed with hiking, biking and horse riding trails.

---

### Hastings Mill Store

1575 Alma St, **T** 7341212. *Mid-Jun-mid-Sep Tue-Sun 1100-1600, otherwise Sat and Sun 1300-1600. By donation. Bus No 9 Broadway or No 4, 7 or 44 to Alma and walk. Map 5, B1, p255*

On the way to UBC, situated on the water near where Alma Street meets Point Grey Road, is the Hastings Mill Store, Vancouver's oldest building, transported from its original site in Gastown. Today it houses a modest museum displaying a small number of First Nations and pioneer artefacts. The building itself is the main event.

---

### ★ Museum of Anthropology

6393 NW Marine Dr, **T** 8225950, www.moa.ubc.ca *Summer daily 1000-1700, Tue until 2100. Winter Wed-Sun 1100-1700, Tue until 2100. $7, $5 seniors, $4 students, children under 6 free. Free entry Tue 1700-2100. Free tours daily at 1100 and 1400, plus 1800 on Tue. Bus No 4 or 10 south on Granville then walk, or change to No 42 at Alma. Parking is the most expensive in town and limited to 2 hrs (which is not enough). Map 1, G1, p249*

Founded in 1949 and situated on Native Musqueam land, this extraordinary museum is easily the best attraction in Vancouver.

The building was designed by Arthur Erickson (see p238) to echo the post-and-beam structures of Northwest Coast First Nations, and contains the world's finest collection of carvings by master craftsmen from many of these Nations, most notably the Haida of Haida Gwaii (Queen Charlotte Islands) and the Gitxsan and Nisga'a from the Skeena River region of Northern BC. The tone is set before you even enter by a pair of traditional but modern **Welcome Figures** and a set of fine red cedar K'san doors. Be sure to pick up a *Gallery Guide* at the Admissions Desk ($1.50). As well as providing a commentary to the exhibits, it gives a brief but excellent introduction to First Nations cultures, the stylistic differences between them and an overview of their classic art forms.

Carvings inside are grouped by general cultural area and informatively labelled. A ramp flanked by works mainly by the local Coast Salish groups quickly leads to the heart of the exhibition, the Great Hall. A 15-m-high wall of glass fills this vast space with ample natural light, whose constantly changing hues and shadows create a perfect atmosphere for the incredible collection of large carvings. Most of the pieces, such as the splendid house posts from Quattishe Village, date from the early- to mid-19th century, but a surprising and encouraging number are very recent. Look out for the painted panels by Lyle Wilson, *Two Salmon*, *Beaver*, and *Killer Whale*; or *Wasco* by Jim Hart. The most exceptional pieces are by the late master **Bill Reid** (see box, p58), such as *Bear* (1963), *Sea Wolf with Killer Whales* (1962) and a 7.5-m inshore cedar canoe (1985). Down the hall a natural-light-filled rotunda houses his most exquisite masterpiece *The Raven and the First Men* (1980), based, like so many of his works, on Haida mythology. Four adjacent cases contain many of his earlier, smaller works.

**!** Vancouver might be the largest port on America's West Coast, but just a century ago people could shout across Burrard Inlet for a ferry to come and pick them up.

### Bill Reid

Born in Vancouver to a Haida mother and Scottish-American father, Bill Reid (1920-98) was a teenager before he was told about his Native heritage. Though he only began investigating Haida arts at the age of 31, he was clearly to the manner born, and his carvings in gold, silver, argillite and wood, castings in bronze, and many book illustrations, have brought him an unparalleled level of recognition. Anthropologist Edmund Carpenter wrote: "I've followed Bill Reid's career for many years and come to believe that, in some strange way, the spirit of Haida art, once the lifeblood of an entire people, now survives within him, at a depth and with an intensity, unrelated to any 'revival' or 'preservation', but deriving from primary sources and leading to daring innovations." In Vancouver, the works of this great artist are to be found at the airport, outside the Aquarium, and above all in the UBC Museum of Anthropology.

The museum has such a large collection of smaller carvings in gold, silver, argillite and wood, that they are constantly rotated. Look out for the excellent late-19th-century silverwork of Charles Edenshaw and the wonderful modern bronze sculptures of Dempsey Bob. Outside, a path leads to a number of exterior exhibits that are visible through the Great Hall's vast windows. This includes a large Haida family dwelling, a smaller mortuary house, and a collection of ten totem poles. There are fine views from here of the city, mountains and ocean below.

Unbelievably, this is still only about half of what the museum has on display. The **Koerner Ceramics Gallery** features a collection of some 1,600 rare European ceramics. At least four galleries are devoted to excellent temporary exhibitions. Then there are the **Visible Storage** galleries: in a relatively small space the museum makes over 14,000 objects accessible to the public, about 40% of its permanent collection. Quality pieces from all over the world, copious enough to fill another large museum, are grouped according to location and huddled together in crammed display cases or pull-out drawers. Again, Canadian aboriginal groups are well represented, including a good collection of Inuit tools and carvings. The sheer quantity of items is overwhelming, so don't dream of trying to take it all in. At least two visits are required to do the museum justice. Try to save a bit of energy for the small gift shop in the lobby which is packed with splendid books, carvings, jewellery and prints.

## Nitobe Memorial Garden and UBC Botanical Garden

*6804 SW Marine Dr, **T** 8229666, www.hedgerows.com  Daily 1000-1800. Nitobe closed weekends in winter. $6 for both, $4.75 for Botanical Garden alone, $2.75 for Nitobe. Students $2. Free tours Wed and Sat 1300. Bus No 4 or 10 south on Granville.  Map 1, G1, p249*

A short stroll from the museum is the Nitobe Memorial Garden, an authentic Japanese tea garden. It is a subtle experience, with every rock, tree and pool playing its part in the delicate harmony to create an ambience that encourages reflection and meditation. There are cherry blossoms in spring, Japanese irises in summer, and Japanese maples in autumn. Moving anti-clockwise, the garden apparently represents the stages of a person's life.

A further 3 km south on Marine Drive is the much more extensive but equally delightful UBC Botanical Garden, the oldest of its kind in Canada. Spread over 28 ha are a number of expertly maintained theme gardens. The Physick Garden is devoted to traditional medicinal plants from 16th-century Europe. The Food Garden provides an instructive lesson from green-fingered experts, including a collection of fruit trees that have been cleverly twisted into various shapes, including a 'UBC'. This is as much an educational as an aesthetic experience, with well-labelled exhibits and regular lectures. The gift shop has many fine gardening-related products and plants for sale.

# South and East Vancouver

*The broad swathe of Vancouver south of False Creek/Burrard Inlet contains only a couple of sights, namely **Queen Elizabeth Park**, which has the **Bloedel Conservatory**, and the pretty **VanDusen Botanical Garden**. For those who know the city, however, there are a handful of small neighbourhoods which are more interesting and reveal more of what the city is really about than the boutiques on Robson Street. This is where you go to savour shops, bars, restaurants and atmosphere. **West Broadway** contains pockets of interest other than the Kitsilano stretch, while **Commercial Drive** and **Main Street** are delightfully gritty, bohemian and cosmopolitan. The latter leads south to Vancouver's **Indiatown**. Further out at the extreme corner of the uninteresting suburb of Richmond is **Steveston**, a picturesque fishing village that still harbours the biggest fishing fleet on Canada's Pacific Coast.*

▸▸ *See Sleeping p110, Eating and drinking p143, Bars and clubs p166*

 ## Sights

### VanDusen Botanical Garden

5251 Oak St and 37th Av, **T** 8789274, www.vandusengarden.org *Daily 1000-2100 Jun-mid-Aug, 1000-2000 May and mid-Aug-mid-Sep, 1000-1800 Apr and late Sep, 1000-1600 Oct-Mar. $5, $3.50 concessions, $2 children, family ticket $11. Bus No 17 on Burrard or Pender. Map 1, H3, p249*

This 22-ha garden, originally purchased from the Canadian Pacific Railway by locals keen to ensure that it was not developed for housing, contains over 7,500 different plants from around the world, including some rare species. Set around lakes, ponds and waterfalls and dotted with sculptures, its 40-odd small theme gardens are considerably more romantic and contemplative than those at UBC. As well as a few suggested walking routes, self-guiding sheets change with the seasons to take visitors around those plants that are at their peak. Early spring is the best overall time. A perennial favourite with kids is the Elizabethan hedge maze. Courses and lectures on various aspects of gardening and botany are offered year round. In December the gardens host the *Festival of Lights*.

---

## Queen Elizabeth Park

Cambie-Ontario Sts and 29-37 Avs, Bloedel Conservatory: **T** 2578570, *Apr-Sep Mon-Fri 0900-2000, Sat and Sun 1000-2100. Oct-Mar 1000-1730. $4, $3 concessions. Bus No 15 on Burrard or Robson. Map 6, F5, p256*

Named in honour of the Queen Mother, this 53-ha park on Cambie and 33rd Avenue, is the former site of two basalt quarries, now converted into ornamental gardens, which make for very pleasant (and free) summer strolling. Along with an extensive rose garden, there is an arboretum said to contain a specimen of almost every tree found in Canada, including some rare species like the giant dogwood. There's also a roller rink, pitch and putt golf, tennis courts, and a nine-basket disk-golf course. Paths lead past a t'ai chi area and a bizarre Henry Moore sculpture to mark Vancouver's highest point (150 m), the peak of an extinct volcano, with good if rather obstructed views of the city below. Arguably the best vistas in town are reserved for patrons of the wonderfully romantic *Seasons in the Park* restaurant (see Eating, p143), which hosted a summit lunch for Bill Clinton and Boris Yeltsin. Nearby is the park's major draw, the **Bloedel Conservatory**, a giant dome that contains 500 varieties of exotic plants from tropical rainforest, subtropical, and desert ecosystems, as well as floral displays that change with the seasons and about 160 free-flying tropical birds.

## Main Street
*Bus No 3 on Seymour or Hastings.  Map 6, A7-F7, p256*

Mixed in among the antique and second-hand stores, trendy but gritty little cafés and restaurants are starting to appear on Main Street, south of 6th Avenue. Further south, between 48th and 50th Avenues, is Vancouver's Indiatown, also known as the **Punjabi Market** (see p147). Here you will find all-you-can-eat buffets, Bollywood music, silk and gold and even the odd *pan walla*. Check out the splendid **Sikh Temple** at 8000 Ross Street, another Arthur Erickson special.

## Commercial Drive
*Bus No 20 on Seymour or Pender, or Broadway SkyTrain.  Map 1, G4-H4, p249*

Once it moves far enough east from the seedy East Side district, Hastings Street loses little of its rough and ready nature, but becomes notably more multicultural and presentable, with some great cheap eateries and ethnic bakeries. It soon connects with Commercial Drive, arguably Vancouver's most worthwhile neighbourhood. Once known as Little Italy, 'The Drive' still retains a number of little Italian coffee shops, but has long since become a much more widely cosmopolitan area that also attracts many of the city's bohemian, artistic, alternative or just plain less wealthy citizens. There are no 'sights' as such, but it's a fascinating place to wander, eat, drink and people watch.

## Steveston Gulf of Georgia Cannery National Historic Site
12138 4th Av, **T** 6649009, www.gulfofgeorgiacannery.com
*1000-1700, daily Jun-Aug, Thu-Mon Apr-May and Sep-Oct, pre-booked tours only Mar and Nov. $6.50, $5 concessions, $3.25 children. Bus No 401, 406 or 407 south on Howe.  Map 1, K3, p249*

South of the Fraser River, far from Downtown but close to the airport, Richmond is flat as a pancake, an ugly, sprawling suburb of malls and megastores. In its southwest corner is Steveston, which has been a fishing village for over a century and still boasts the largest commercial fishing fleet on Canada's Pacific shore. In 1901, when over 10,000 people crowded its boardwalks and saloons, the village's 50 or so canneries set a record by shipping out a staggering 16 million pounds of salmon. A reminder of those heady days and Steveston's biggest sight is the Gulf of Georgia Cannery National Historic Site, nicknamed the 'Monster'. Tours of the site include the *Journey Through Time* multimedia presentation, 10,000 artefacts and machinery dating back to 1900.

Nearby are the restored **Britannia Heritage Shipyards**, the oldest remaining structures on the Fraser River. When the boat comes in, the sea's bounty can be bought directly from fishing boats at the public fish sales dock. At 3811 Moncton Street is the small **Steveston Museum**, which is easily missed. The village's real appeal resides in its salty seaside atmosphere, though high numbers of tourists in the summer can take the edge off the experience. The best strolling is along **Bayview Street** between No 1 Road and 3rd Avenue, where a number of outside tables at the many restaurants make for romantic dining on a summer evening.

---

### Buddhist Temple
9160 Steveston Hwy, **T** 2742822, www.BuddhistTemple.org  *Daily 0930-1700. Free. Bus No 403 on Howe (50 mins).  Map 1, K4, p249*

Once you've come this far, it's worth considering a lengthy diversion to the incredible Buddhist Temple, justifiably vaunted as one of the finest examples of Chinese palatial architecture on the continent. Built in the late 1970s, its spectacular exterior, with golden porcelain tiles and flying dragons on the roof, and marble lions guarding the foot of the stairway, is only surpassed by the sumptuous interior. Outside is a Classical Chinese garden, twin

## Hikes around the North Shore

**Mount Gardner**, 16-km round trip, 750-m elevation gain. Trailhead: take the ferry from Horseshoe bay to Bowen Island. Directions are complicated so ask at the Information Centre. A tough but highly rewarding hike that's possible almost year round. Be sure to catch an early ferry to allow plenty of time. Panoramic views from the top are spectacular.

**Hollyburn Mountain**, 8-km round trip, 405-m elevation gain. Trailhead: by the ski area map next to the parking lot in Cypress Provincial Park. Excellent, fairly easy trail leading to great views. Leads through probably the finest stand of ancient, giant cedar, fir and hemlock within reach of the city. Usually snow-free mid-June to mid-November.

**Mount Strachan**, 10-km round trip, 534-m elevation gain. Trailhead: as above. This route follows the Howe Sound Crest Trail for a while before heading through Strachan Meadows then steeply up the edge of a gorge, alongside precipitous cliffs and through a beautiful stretch of old-growth forest. The north summit offers the best views. This trail is rarely free of snow before mid-July.

**Mount Seymour**, 9-km round trip, 440-m elevation gain. Trailhead: Mount Seymour Provincial Park parking lot. A fairly quick route to some of the most extensive panoramas of all, but no pushover: the route can be confusing, and is dangerously exposed to bad weather. Rarely snow-free before August.

gazebos, fountains, pools and sculptures, and a lovely courtyard with a ceramic mural. Look out for the bronze incense burner, the row of Tang Dynasty lanterns, and the 22-m-long Seven Buddha Mural. Buddhist ceremonies, lectures and meditation classes are held, as well as art exhibitions.

# North Shore

*For many people, Vancouver's North Shore represents its finest feature. The mountains that provide so stunning a backdrop to Downtown make for excellent recreational possibilities, including skiing, hiking, kayaking and mountain biking in a string of outstanding semi-wilderness parks and valleys. Locals started canoeing across the water for a breath of fresh air as early as the 1880s, but the first residential areas were only established after the Guinness Company bought 4,000 acres of land there in 1931 and built the **Lion's Gate Bridge** across the First Narrows. Modelled on San Francisco's Golden Gate, this was the Empire's longest suspension bridge in 1938. Today the districts collectively known as the North Shore are inhabited by the city's wealthy, whose per capita earnings are the highest in Canada. Beside the major parks, however, there is little interest or culture here beyond a clutch of small galleries and a few decent neighbourhood pubs. The obvious way to arrive is on the SeaBus, which docks at **Lonsdale Quay Market**, the North Shore's only real focal point. Local buses continue from there. The glazed and galleried interior of the market is a throwback to 19th-century industrial architecture, and well worth a look, but this is no real alternative to Granville Island.*

▸▸ *See Eating and drinking p148, Bars and clubs p167*

  Sights

### Capilano Suspension Bridge

3735 Capilano Rd, **T** 9857474, www.capbridge.com *Summer 0830-dusk, winter 0900-1700. $9.35, $6 concessions, $3 parking. Bus No 246 from Georgia or No 236 from Lonsdale Quay. Map 1, E4, p248*

Almost due north from Lion's Gate Bridge, Capilano Road runs parallel to the eponymous river, valley and regional park all the way to the dammed Capilano Lake and beyond to Grouse Mountain.

**Walking in the Sky**
*A suspension bridge has spanned the Capilano River for over a century; this one is the longest and highest of its kind in the world.*

Capilano Suspension Bridge is Vancouver's oldest and most vaunted attraction. The current bridge is the fourth to span the 137 m across Capilano River 70 m below, which apparently makes it the longest and highest suspended footbridge in the world. The first was built in 1889 by land developer George Grant Mackay, who knew a beautiful spot when he saw one, and bought up 6,000 acres along the river. Beyond a small collection of totem poles, a diminutive First Nations carving shed and a few photos and artefacts, there is little to justify the entrance fee besides the admittedly astounding natural beauty and the short-lived excitement of walking across the bridge. Beyond is a patch of forest best described as manicured, with some very short trails through giant trees. The Living Forest interactive exhibit is aimed at kids, with educational facts and displays of dead bugs.

### Capilano River Regional Park
*Map 1, E3, p248*

For a free and more genuine taste of the valley's natural beauty, head up the road to the 160-ha Capilano River Regional Park. Access is from several car parks along Capilano Park Road, which heads west from Capilano Road shortly after the suspension bridge, or directly from the latter at Cleveland Dam. Sitting on Capilano Lake and supplying much of Vancouver's drinking water, the dam offers fine views of the Coast Mountains. The park protects Capilano River as it heads south to Burrard Inlet, a journey followed by the 7.5-km one-way **Capilano Pacific Trail**, the longest of 10 trails of the unmanicured variety. Trail maps are available at car park information boards or from Information Centres, and outline a number of pools and other river features to look out for. The park also contains the **Capilano Salmon Hatchery** (**T** 6661790, free), one of the best places to see them run, with panels recounting the whole story.

**Grouse Mountain**
*Everything from skiing to ice-skating, sleigh rides to paragliding, pub grub to fine dining; and all just a stone's throw from the city.*

## ★ Grouse Mountain

**T** 9840661, www.grousemtn.com  *Gondola runs every 15 mins year-round 0900-2200, $20, $18 seniors, $13 13-18 year olds, $8 5-12 year olds, under 5s free. SeaBus then Bus No 236 from Lonsdale Quay  Map 1, D4, p248*

The lights of Grouse Mountain, the most popular and easily reached **ski hill** on the North Shore, seem to hang from Vancouver's night-time skyline like Christmas tree decorations. Skiing here was pioneered as early as 1911 and the first double chairlift in North America was built in 1949. Today skiers and sightseers are whisked up to 1,100 m above sea level in about 8 minutes by the **SkyRide Gondola**. At the top are year-round panoramic views, 16-ft chain-saw sculptures and a host of activities and facilities. The atmosphere is wonderful between December-April when thousands of city-dwellers flock in to enjoy downhill skiing and snowboarding, ice skating, sleigh rides, 10 km of snow-shoeing, and 5 km of cross-country skiing (see p205). In summer there is hiking (though not the best), mountain biking, paragliding, helicopter tours ($75-110) and horse-drawn carriage rides (the horses also come up in the gondolas). The *Theatre in the Sky* shows a 30-minute multimedia film that is free with the gondola pass.

Facilities at the lodge include everything apart from accommodation. There are a couple of upmarket restaurants (see p148) as well as a fairly basic cafeteria, *Lupins*, and the drinking spot, *Bar 98*, which has great views and pub food. *Alpine Guest Services* in the lodge give information and will store bags. All manner of lessons are available and equipment can be rented. There's even an ATM.

## Cypress Provincial Park

**T** 8789229, www.cypressmountain.com   *Shuttle bus from Lonsdale Quay or Horseshoe Bay.   Map 1, D2, p248*

The next park west of Grouse Mountain is Cypress, whose access road can be seen ascending the mountainous terrain in wide, drunken zig-zags. This has been a popular recreation site since the 1920s and offers the same range of summer and winter activities as Grouse Mountain, though with less extensive facilities and thinner crowds. Some of the North Shore's best hikes are here (see box, p64), leading to panoramic views that take in the city, Howe Sound, lofty Mount Baker to the southeast and the Gulf Islands, Georgia Strait and Vancouver Island to the west. Pick up a blue *BC Parks* map from the main Information Centre.

## Lighthouse Park

*Bus No 250 from Downtown.   Map 1, F1, p248*

West again from Cypress Provincial Park, this small 75-ha park is one of the most accessible and best for strolling, and it contains some of the most rugged and striking forest on the North Shore, including one of the last remaining stands of old-growth Douglas firs. A number of short trails lead to arbutus trees, cliffs and the Point Atkinson Lighthouse, which has been staffed continuously since 1875. Today it can be seen, but not reached.

## Bowen Island

*Ferries from Horseshoe Bay leave roughly hourly from 0600-2125.*
Map 1, D1, p248

Highway 1/99 swings north towards Squamish, soon passing Horseshoe Bay (Bus No 250 or 257 on Georgia), the terminal for ferries to Nanaimo, and a surprisingly pretty village in its own right. The closest excursion to offer a taste of the more laid-back pace of life on the Gulf Islands is Bowen Island, a mere 20 minutes away but already a different world, its 3,500 population characteristically including a large number of writers and artists. Just off the ferry landing is the main centre of **Snug Cove**. The renovated *Union Steamship Company General Store* now houses an Information Centre, where you can pick up a free copy of the *Bowen Island Book* brochure, with a map and a complete list of places to eat, accommodation and activities. Ask also for the free *Happy Island Historic Walking Tour*, a reference to the name given to the island by romancing couples who sailed over in the 1930s and 40s to visit the largest dance pavilion in BC. Nearby is *Doc Morgan's Inn*, a popular spot for a pint and pub food, with an outdoor patio and views of the marina and Cypress Mountain. Many people come for the fine **boating** and **kayaking**, which benefit greatly from the sheltered bays that surround this 50-sq-km island. Mount Gardner is an excellent 16-km return **day-hike** that is possible almost year-round (see hikes, p64).

## Lynn Valley

*For Lynn Canyon Park, exit 19 from Hwy 1 or bus No 229 from Lonsdale Quay; for Lynn Headwaters Regional Park, bus No 228 from Lonsdale Quay gets you closest.* Map 1, E6, p248

Moving east from the Lion's Gate Bridge and Lonsdale Quay, the nearest attraction is Lynn Valley, which is protected by a number of parks. The closest, reached via Lynn Valley Road, is **Lynn Canyon Park**, 250 ha of relatively unspoilt forest. The **Ecology Centre**, by the parking zone at 3663 Peters Road, *daily 1000-1700, but closed weekends Dec and Jan*, has displays, films and plenty of information about the park, as well as a free map and guided walks. The 68-m suspension bridge that hovers 50 m above the rushing waters of Lynn Creek is free. Many **hiking** trails of varying length begin on the other side, including a 15-minute stroll to a wooden footbridge that crosses the creek at Twin Falls.

Longer hikes lead into two much bigger, more remote chunks of protected forest. At the very end of Lynn Valley Road is **Lynn Headwaters Regional Park**, 4,685 ha of second-growth forest with 41 km of well-signed and maintained hiking trails, varying from short strolls along the creek to full-on backcountry treks (see Sports). A **Visitor Centre**, **T** 4326350, is open in summer for information and trail maps. **Seymour Demonstration Forest** (drivers follow Lillooet Road north past Capilano College and cemetery) contains 5,600 ha of interpretive trails through trees that are second growth but still massive, their girth intended to show that with proper management logging need not result in ugly clear-cuts and sad tree farms. The best of some 50 km of hiking and biking trails is the 22-km round-trip to the enormous, very dramatic Seymour Dam. There are also plenty of swimming holes where you can cool off in summer and a 15-m-long Indian war canoe built in 1921.

**!** The tallest tree ever measured on Earth was a 120-m Douglas fir in Lynn Valley.

## Mount Seymour Provincial Park

*Shuttle for the ski hill, winter only (see Sports). Map 1, E6, p248*

Mount Seymour Road leaves Mount Seymour Parkway at the
eastern end of the North Shore and climbs steeply up 1,000 vertical
metres passing two stunning viewpoints, both worth a stop.
Mount Seymour was first climbed in 1908, skiing first attempted
by members of the Alpine Club in 1929 and the 3,508-ha park
established in 1936. Other than the commercial ski hill, the park's
semi-wilderness old-growth forest and sub-alpine wildflower
meadows make for some excellent hiking (see Sports). Pick up a
blue *BC Parks* map from the main Information Centre. Flower Lake
Loop is a pleasant 1.5-km stroll through bog and ponds, a good
place for spotting birds.

## Deep Cove

*SeaBus then Bus No 229 to Phibbs Exchange then bus No 211 or 212.
Map 1, F7, p248*

A lovely picturesque spot with views across the bay to snowy hills
beyond, Deep Cove retains the unspoilt feel of a seaside village.
As well as the starting point for mountain biking and Vancouver's
best kayaking up **Indian Arm** (see Sports, p203), it has a nice
green park by the water, a few good restaurants and the best
neighbourhood pub in town.

Listings

### Museums and galleries

- **Canadian Craft and Design Museum** Innovative exhibits of artisan expertise in various media, p36.
- **Chinese Cultural Centre Museum** Recounts the story of Canadian Chinese from the Gold Rush to the present, p44.
- **Granville Island Sport Fishing, Model Ships and Model Trains museums** Three small but superlative museums in one. An absolute must for anyone with even a passing interest, p52.
- **Maritime Museum** Lots of items, including the entire *RCMP St Roch*, the first ship to negotiate the Arctic 'Northwest Passage', p53.
- **Gulf of Georgia Cannery National Historic Site** The last operating and biggest cannery on BC's coast, full of artefacts and old machinery, p62.
- **Hastings Mill Store** The city's oldest building, housing a modest collection of First Nations and pioneer artefacts, p56.
- **Museum of Anthropology** Vancouver's best attraction, with exceptional displays of First Nations carving and artefacts from around the world, p56.
- **Pacific Mineral Museum** 848 W Hastings, www.pacific mineralmuseum.org Large collection of meteorites, fossils and gems. The gift shop sells more of the same, p74.
- **Roedde House Museum** House built in 1893, furnished in Edwardian style, p45.
- **Vancouver Museum** Rather dull walk through Vancouver's history, p52.
- **Vancouver Art Gallery** Temporary exhibitions spread over four spacious floors of an impressive neoclassical building. Permanent exhibition of works by Victoria artist Emily Carr, p33.

## Squamish and Garibaldi Provincial Park  77
The country's best rock-climbing, windsurfing and bald eagle-watching.  Fine hiking trails, awesome scenery, soaring peaks, pristine lakes, alpine meadows and colossal glaciers.

## Whistler  79
North America's most celebrated ski resort, two hours from the city. In summer, it's a Mecca for all kinds of outdoor activities.

## Victoria  82
A picturesque little town, British Columbia's capital, with flower gardens, scenic harbour location and grandiose architecture. A fine museum, lots for kids and some great restaurants and bars.

## Tofino and around  89
An attractive seaside village and base for whale-watching and a host of other trips and hikes.

## Gulf Islands: Galiano and Salt Spring  94
This archipelago is famous for its laid-back pace, artistic and bohemian inhabitants.

# Sea to Sky Highway

The Sea to Sky Highway is the apt and popular name for Highway 99, a gorgeous drive which follows Howe Sound north from Vancouver's Horseshoe Bay first to **Squamish**, then up through the gloriously scenic **Coast Mountains** to **Garibaldi Provincial Park** and **Whistler**.

## Squamish and Garibaldi Provincial Park

*Despite its extraordinary mountain-ringed location, Squamish is not much to look at and, with one notable exception, its facilities are very poor. Yet for the outdoor enthusiast, this is a veritable Mecca. Meaning 'Mother of the wind' in Coast Salish, Squamish has come to be recognized as the country's **windsurfing** capital. There's also excellent **hiking** and **mountain biking**, and plenty of fishing and kayaking. Once you get beyond the sprawl emanating from Squamish, the journey to Whistler is a delight, giving an idea of the incredible scenery contained within Garibaldi Provincial Park to the east.*

▸▸ *See also Sleeping p114, Eating and drinking p149, Sports p207*

---

*Frequent buses from Vancouver bus station, also steam train May-Sep leaves North Vancouver at 1000 and takes two hours. By boat, MV Brittania leaves Vancouver Harbour at 0930 and takes three hours.*
*See also p21*

---

##  Sights

---

**Stawamus Chief**
*Map, inside back cover*

Above all, Squamish is famous for its climbing, with some 200,000 international hopefuls visiting annually to take on the 95-million-year-old Stawamus Chief, the second biggest granite monolith on

Earth, and an awesome spectacle towering over the Squamish sprawl. Those same massive rock walls that are so good to climb also act as a funnel, channelling the Howe Sound's perpetually strong ocean winds straight into town.

The mighty chief is not just for climbers. It makes a great hike to fantastic views that is within the capabilities of occasional hikers, and it is snow-free as early as March and as late as November. Most people make for the first (south) of the three summits, so try heading for the second or third, or even hike to them all. Descending is more fun via the second summit than the East trail (6-11-km round trip, 612-m elevation gain. Trailhead: Shannon Falls Provincial Park, just south of Squamish, or 1.2 km further north).

Another worthwhile hike is to **High Falls Creek** (12-km round trip, 640-m elevation gain). Ten and a half kilometres north of Squamish take the Squamish Valley Road. At Km 24.2 stay right on Squamish River Road. Park at Km 3.1 and look for sign 100 m further on the right. As well as falls and gorges, this sometimes steep route offers views of the glacier-clad Tantalus Range. Continue as far as the logging road and descend to make a loop; first-class views compensate for the lack of trail aesthetics.

---

## Brackendale

*10 km north of Squamish.*  Map, inside back cover

Brackendale is visited by more **bald eagles** than any other place on earth. Attracted by the spawning salmon, an estimated 10,000 of these majestic birds stop by every winter, now protected by the creation of the 550-ha Brackendale Eagles Provincial Park. The best places to get more information are the **Brackendale Art Gallery** on Government Road, north of Depot Road, **T** 8983333, www.brackendaleartgallery.com, and the **Sunwolf Outdoor Centre** at 70002 Squamish Valley Road, 4 km off the Sea to Sky Highway, **T** 8981537, www.sunwolf.net  The latter has 10 riverside cabins and arranges eagle-watching trips by raft and kayak.

**Canadian Outback Adventure Co**, **T** 1800-5658735, also offer eagle-watching river-raft trips with transport from Vancouver. Incorporating the official Eagle Count, the **Brackendale Winter Eagles Festival** will enjoy its 18th year in January 2004.

### ★ Garibaldi Provincial Park

*Close to Highway 99, between Squamish and Whistler; entry is mainly on foot, for hiking trails see p80.* Map, inside back cover

This is the nearest thing to a wilderness park you'll find within such easy reach of a major city and two prime sporting Meccas. Too popular for some people's taste, it still boasts magnificent scenery, and hiking is some of the best in the country along trails that are clearly signed and well maintained. Walk-in campsites are primitive and tend to be self-registration, so take some cash.

# Whistler

*Whistler is the largest ski area in North America and is consistently voted the continent's number one ski resort. The terrain is vast, the facilities state-of-the-art, and the management bend over backwards to make sure the visitor's every need is anticipated. Many other winter sports are available and in summer the gondola whisks hikers up to instant effortless alpine views.* Map inside back cover

▸▸ *See also Sleeping p115, Eating and drinking p150, Sports p115*

*Bus station, 4338 Main St, **T** 9325031. Greyhound buses and several other shuttles run between the airport and hotels in Vancouver and Whistler. A free shuttle runs around the village and to the gondola all day. Tourist Information Centre, Highway 99 at Lake Placid Rd, **T** 9325528, www.mywhistler.com, and a more useful Activity and Info Centre, in the Conference Centre at the Whistler Way end of the Village. For skiing information **T** 9323434, www.whistler-blackcomb.com*

## ▶ Hikes along the Sea to Sky Highway

First-class hiking is found throughout the Coast Mountain Range. From south to north these are the very best trails: **Stawamus Chief**, 6, 9 or 11 km round trip, 612-m elevation gain. Trailhead: Shannon Falls, just south of Squamish, or 1.2 km further north. A great hike to fantastic views that's not too demanding, and usually snow-free March-November. **Garibaldi Lake/Taylor Meadows**, 35 km round trip (max), 2,450-m elevation gain. Trailhead: Rubble Creek. 38 km north of Squamish, or 20 km south of Whistler, turn east at Black Tusk sign and proceed 2.6 km. A highly rewarding hiking zone, with many possible itineraries. Garibaldi Lake is huge, vividly coloured and surrounded by superb views. Camp here or at the broad, flower-strewn Taylor Meadows a few kilometres away. Highly recommended side-trips run to Panorama Ridge, with monster views of ice and peaks, and to Black Tusk, a distinctive volcanic peak. **Brandywine Meadows**, 13.6 km round trip, 600-m elevation gain. Trailhead: 15 km south of Whistler, 44 km north of Squamish, turn west onto Brandywine Forestry Road. Park on left at Km 4.4. A popular hike to an alpine bowl full of wildflower meadows (best in early August) and set beneath towering cliffs. **Cheakamus Lake**, 6.4 km

## ◉ Sights

The purpose-built Whistler Village is a toy-town maze of fancy hotels, bars, restaurants and sport stores, whose Legoland appearance could attract or repel depending on your taste and state of mind. The smart decision to keep all traffic out of the centre, leaving pedestrians to stroll at leisure between services, reinforces the impression of being in a holiday-camp, and the return, 12.8-km with a loop of the lake, elevation gain negligible. Trailhead: 7.7 km south of Whistler, 51.3 km north of Squamish, turn east onto a logging road and continue 7.5 km to end. This easy trail leads through patches of old growth forest, to a big, beautiful turquoise lake with ice-covered peaks soaring 1,600 m over its shoreline.

**Blackcomb Peak**, 9 km round trip, 355-m elevation gain. From Whistler Village parking lot take the Fitzsimmons trail and watch for the chairlift icon. Take the chairlift up 1,174 m to Rendezvous Lodge. An easy way to reach dizzying vistas of peaks, glaciers and wildflower meadows.

**Cougar Mountain Cedar Grove**, 5 km round trip, 150-m elevation gain. Trailhead: 5 km north of Whistler turn west onto dirt road for 5 km. This short walk is not special, but the ancient cedars at its end are spectacular and humbling.

**Joffre Lakes**, 11 km, 370-m elevation gain. Trailhead: 30 km north of Pemberton in Joffre Lakes Recreation Area. A relatively easy hike to three gorgeous teal lakes set in exquisite mountain scenery. The first lake is reached after a mere five minutes.

For more information on these and other trails, try Kathy and Craig Copeland's, *Don't Waste Your Time in the BC Coast Mountains*.

perpetual party atmosphere is helped along by several major seasonal festivals, with smaller events almost every weekend.

For skiing, Whistler and Blackcomb Mountains each have their own characters and devotees. Whistler is traditionally more laid back and suitable for beginners and intermediates and has a Family Zone at the *Emerald Express*. The breakdown of terrain for the two hills is very similar at about 15% beginner, 55% intermediate, 30% expert. **Blackcomb** is the one that breaks most of the records, boasting for example the two longest lift-serviced vertical falls in North America. Its Terrain Park is a favourite with snow-boarders and serious experts. For the latter there is also an Expert Park, which you can only enter with a helmet and a special endorsement on your pass.

# Vancouver Island

A short hop across the Strait of Georgia from Vancouver is the largest island on North America's west coast and a prime destination in its own right, especially for outdoor enthusiasts. Two locations here stand out as supreme excursions: Victoria and Tofino. Located on opposite sides of the island, these towns exemplify the extremely distinctive characters of the two coasts.

## Victoria

*British Columbia's capital is also its most charming and atmospheric town, thanks to its waterfront location, remarkably mild climate, and splendid stone and brick buildings. Hemmed in on three sides by water, and liberally scattered with flower gardens and parks, Victoria is a great place for oceanside walks, with orcas often visible right from the shore. The picturesque boat-filled* **Inner Harbour***, lined with Victoria's most impressive architecture, is a wonderfully atmospheric spot. Among its attractions is the* **Royal British Columbia Museum***, which provides an excellent overview of the province. Victoria also has a far better selection of restaurants and bars than you could reasonably expect of a town this size. The only drawback for visitors from the UK is an exaggerated Englishness aimed at American tourists, and many phoney sights are best avoided.* Map, inside back cover

▸▸ *See also Sleeping p117, Eating and drinking p152*

*Easily reached from Vancouver by plane, bus or ferry then car/bike. The bus terminal is Downtown at 700 Douglas St. See also p21 Most*

*major sights can be easily visited on foot and orientation is simple.
A comprehensive bus service operates throughout the city. There are
numerous bike lanes and trails, T 5984556, www.cycling victoria.com
Travel Information Centre, 812 Wharf, Inner Harbour, T 9532033,
www.tourismvictoria.com, 0900-1700, (1830 in summer).*

# Sights

### ★ Royal British Columbia Museum
*675 Belleville St, T 3567226, www.royalbcmuseum.bc.ca  Daily
0900-1700. $10, $7 concessions. Corner of Government St. Helmcken
House  May-Oct 1000-1700, shorter hours the rest of the year. $5, $3
concessions.*

Housed in a modest building to the south of the *Empress*, this fine
museum consists of four permanent exhibitions. Many people's
favourite is the **Open Ocean** exhibit, which uses dark tunnels,
lifts, films and state-of-the-art audiovisual wizardry to take you on
a submarine adventure through the wonders and mysteries of the
sea. Visitors are admitted half-hourly in groups of ten, so take a
time-coded ticket and head on to the **Natural History Gallery**,
where a series of extremely realistic dioramas evoke BC's many
varied and extraordinary landscapes. Set within brilliantly
re-created environments, the animals are so expertly stuffed that
you half expect them to move. Particularly popular is a life-sized
example of the woolly mammoths that roamed these lands until
13,000 years ago.

The **First Peoples Gallery** uses works of art, wooden masks,
carvings, ancient artefacts, original documents, films and
audiovisual displays to recount the full, tragic history of British
Columbia's aboriginal nations. The journey through time is picked
up with an exploration of the white man's world in the **Modern
History Gallery**, which contains as much information on the
province's social history as anyone could want, with countless

artefacts and displays on the gold-rush and early pioneers, plus a re-creation of turn-of-the-last-century Victoria, complete with cobblestone streets, buildings and alleys, and a movie house that shows silent films. The museum also contains the **National Geographic Imax Theatre**, T 4804887, www.imaxvictoria.com

Behind the museum on Elliot Street is **Thunderbird Park** whose collection of modern totem poles complements the First Nations Gallery within. A small carving shed offers the chance to see Native masters at work.

Next door at 10 Elliot Street is **Helmcken House**, the oldest surviving house in BC. Built in 1852 for a pioneer physician, it contains an unusually intact set of frightening 19th-century medical implements, as well as lots of other Victoriana.

## Inner Harbour
Parliament Building, **T** 3873046. *Daily 0830-1700.*

A multitude of assorted craft, from kayaks and ferries to yachts and float-planes, ply these waters where passenger steamships once unloaded their genteel cargo. The wide open space and undeniable grandeur of the surrounding architecture conspire to create a magical ambience, especially in summer when the harbour walkway throngs with art peddlers, buskers and tourists. The view landwards is entirely dominated by Victoria's grandest constructions, three of which were designed by architect Francis Rattenbury (see p237). The **Empress Hotel** was built in 1908 and retains the opulence of the Victorian era splendidly. You can go in and explore the many lounges, lobbies and dining halls, all dripping with colonial excess; maybe have a drink beneath the Tiffany-glass dome of the Crystal Lounge, or join the staggering number who attend the ritual of high tea in the Tea Lounge. Built in 1897, the equally extravagant **Parliament Building** sets the tone for the whole town, especially at night when it's evocatively illuminated by 3,333 tiny lightbulbs. The inside can be visited on a free guided tour, but despite the anecdotes and efforts of the guides, and a few historical artefacts such as the dagger that killed Captain Cook, it's really not as impressive as the exterior.

The Inner Harbour has several minor attractions, most of them geared towards kids: **Miniature World**, 649 Humboldt Street, **T** 3859731, www.miniatureworld.com, features tiny reconstructions of various themes and a scale model of the coast-to-coast Canadian Pacific Railway; **Crystal Gardens**, 713 Douglas Street, **T** 3811213, is a 1925 glassed-in conservatory designed by Rattenbury, containing tropical gardens and 65 different endangered creatures, such as tiny monkeys the size of a finger; the **Royal London Wax Museum**, 470 Belleville Street, **T** 3884461, www.waxworld.com, yet another design by the prolific Rattenbury, has its own mandatory but gruesome Chamber of Horrors; and the **Pacific Undersea Gardens**, 490 Belleville Street, **T** 3825717, www.pacificunderseagardens.com, in front of the Parliament Buildings, is a giant underwater aquarium with instructors who swim and perform alongside a vast array of colourful, bizarre and fascinating ocean-dwellers.

Four blocks behind the Parliament Building, at 207 Government Street, is **Emily Carr House**, *May-Oct 1000-1700, 1200-1600 Feb-Mar, $5.35*. This 1864 house is where the much-loved Canadian painter and writer (see also p237) was born and lived most of her twilight years, surrounded by all sorts of animals. Her paintings are important historically as well as artistically, because she made a visual record of the coastal First Nations of the time. There is a gift shop and a small art gallery showing the work of local artists.

---

## Downtown

*Maritime Museum, 28 Bastion Sq, **T** 3854222, www.mmbc.bc.ca Daily 0930-1630. $6, $2 concessions. Victoria Bug Zoo, 1107 Wharf St, **T** 3842847, www.bugzoo.bc.ca Summer daily 0930-2100; rest of year Mon-Sat 0930-1730, Sun 1100-1730. $6, $5 seniors, $4 children.*

This is Victoria's oldest quarter and if you look up above the tacky gift shops on Government Street with their nasty ground-floor façades, you'll discover some fine brick and stone buildings. Check out, for example, the art nouveau-style tobacconists at No 1116. While here, be sure to have a look in Hill's at No 1006 whose wide selection of First Nations masks, carvings and jewellery is one of the best you'll see.

● *For first-class restaurants and bars – the area's real attraction – wander down adjacent streets like Yates (see p152).*

Near Bastion Square is **Victoria Bug Zoo**, an off-beat but strangely compelling collection of weird and wonderful insects from around the world. Concentrated around Fisgard Street and the absurdly named Gate of Harmonious Interest is the oldest **Chinatown** in Canada, where eating is the main event. Fan Tan Alley, former red-light district and the narrowest street in Canada, has some nice little shops to explore.

**Bastion Square**, site of the original Fort Victoria, is pleasant enough, but there's little to see except the handsome former provincial courthouse which today houses the **Maritime Museum**. Several exhibition spaces here contain myriad artefacts from the Pacific Northwest's maritime history, highlight of which is the *Tillikum*, the dug-out canoe in which Captain John Voss made his three-year attempt to circumnavigate the globe in 1901.

## Beacon Hill Park and the Coast
*Open 24 hours daily. Free. Bus No 5 or No 11.*

To reach the third key area of Victoria, follow Douglas Street south to the ocean and the beautiful Beacon Hill Park, where you will see the results of Victoria's wonderful climate. Winding paths pass all kinds of trees, from mighty old-growth giants to ornamental deciduous species, past duck-ponds, swans and roaming peacocks, between gardens where tens of thousands of flowers are lovingly tended and arranged. There are also some excellent free **tennis** courts, **lawn** bowling, a **soccer** field and a **cricket** pitch, as well as a petting zoo for children, *mid-Mar-mid-Oct, by donation*. From here it is a lovely stroll along the ocean, with many good viewpoints and trails down to the rock pools. Those with a vehicle or bike should follow the coast east along Dallas Road, taking the scenic routes and admiring the grand houses, maybe as far as the genteel community of **Oak Bay**. Orcas can sometimes be seen from the oceanfront along Dallas Road. To get closer, there are plenty of operators desperate to take you **whale-watching**.

### ★ Butchart Gardens

Keating Rd, **T** 6525256, www.butchartgardens.com  *Daily 0900-2230 in summer, earlier in winter. $18 ($14 off-season), $7 concessions, $2 children. 20 km north of Victoria, 20 km south of ferry. Follow red signs west from Highway 17. Central Saanich bus route No 75 from Douglas St, or Laidlaw bus (9 daily, T 3854411).*

By far the most celebrated of Victoria's gardens, these cover 20 ha and include Japanese, rose, Italian, and sunken gardens. Beautiful in any season, the gardens are spectacularly illuminated at night. Stunning firework displays set to music take place on Saturday evenings in July and August at no extra cost, and there's often live music and puppet shows. The site contains a gift shop, restaurant, coffee shop and a dining room serving high tea.

   ● *While this far out, you might as well head three minutes south to 1461 Benvenuto Road and take in the **Butterfly Gardens**, daily Mar-Sep 0900-1700, $8.75, $7.75 seniors, $5 children, an indoor conservatory packed with colourful 'critters' that flutter by.*

### Abkhazi Gardens

1964 Fairfield Rd, **T** 4798053, www.conservancy.bc.ca  *Mar-Oct 1300-1600, Wed-Fri and Sun. $8, $4.50 concessions suggested donation. Bus No 7 from town.*

A closer, cheaper, but much smaller alternative to Butchart is the Abkhazi Gardens, a gorgeous property created by Prince and Princess Abkhazi in the 1940s and recently saved from housing developers through a purchase by the Land Conservancy. The upper garden affords great views of Victoria and the Juan de Fuca Strait.

## Craigdarroch Castle

1050 Joan Crescent, **T** 5925323, *0900-1900 in summer, 1000-1630 in winter. $10, $5.50 concessions, $2.50 children. Off Fort St. Bus No 11 or 14 from Downtown.*

If you still have time, a few reasonable sights are clustered together not far east of Downtown in an area called Rockland. Of these, the most interesting is Craigdarroch Castle, which was built in 1887-89 by Robert Dunsmuir, a Scottish mining expert who was drafted in to help exploit the black seams further north in Nanaimo and ended up discovering the most productive coal mine in North America. Thanks to a shrewd business sense and utter lack of scruples, he became BC's first millionaire, his net worth mounting to $20 million by the time he died. Ironically, this happened just six months before his castle was completed. If you visit one historical building in Victoria, make it this one. The rooms are exquisitely furnished, with magnificent stained glass, immaculate Victorian furnishings and ornaments, and a few oddities like a 3-D picture made entirely out of human hair. Be sure to linger over the first few rooms, as these are the best.

## Art Gallery of Greater Victoria

1040 Moss St, **T** 3844101, www.aggv.bc.ca *Mon-Sat 1000-1700, Thu 1000-2100, Sun 1300-1700, $5, $3 concessions, under 12s free; donation only on Mon. East of Downtown off Fort St. Bus No 11, 22 or 14.*

> **Clayoquot Sound**
>
> In 1993, the Canadian government gave logging companies the go-ahead to chop down two-thirds of British Columbia's rainforest and sparked the largest civil disobedience action in Canadian history, led by environmentalists and Native Americans. The protest caught the world's attention, and resulted in a temporary victory for the activists. However, two companies still retain significant logging rights in the Sound and *The Friends of Clayoquot Sound*, 331 Neill Street, **T** 7254218, www.island.net~focs, continue with the struggle.

Victoria's main Art Gallery is less impressively housed than Vancouver's, and far more likely to appeal to those whose tastes do not run to modern art. Its extensive permanent collection is constantly rotated and includes a massive store of Japanese art as well as quite a few of Emily Carr's less distinguished works (see p237). There are always a few visiting exhibitions too, so most people should find something they like.

● *While in the area you might also want to take a stroll around the 6 ha of ornamental gardens at **Government House**, 1401 Rockland Avenue, **T** 3872080 (bus No 1); this is where the British Royal Family stays when visiting.*

# Tofino and around

*Relentlessly lashed by the ill-named ocean, and barely populated at all as a result, Vancouver Island's West Coast is ruggedly beautiful, blessed with giant trees and thousands of migrating whales. Situated at the heart of **Pacific Rim National Park**, Tofino offers many exciting opportunities to discover this wild domain. The overwhelming popularity of this former whaling-station owes much*

**Rapid action**
*It's not all skiing: paddling around the Gulf Islands, near Tofino, or up the 18-km fjord of India Arm is about as good as it gets.*

to its formidable location. Sitting at the end of a narrow peninsula in the middle of beautiful **Clayoquot Sound**, surrounded on all sides by ocean and scenic islands, it is also the closest base for exploring the endless shoreline of **Long Beach**. A handful of superb excursions lead to outstanding destinations like **Hot Springs Cove**, one of the finest remaining stands of giant old-growth trees on **Meares Island**, or an encounter with aboriginal culture on **Flores Island**. Other local activities include whale-watching, unparallelled sea-kayaking, hiking, bear-watching, beachcombing, the country's best surfing, and the increasingly popular recreation of storm-watching.

Despite being packed to the gills throughout the summer, Tofino itself just about manages to remain a scenic seaside village, and for most people its happy holiday resort atmosphere only adds to the experience. There's also a much finer selection of restaurants, cafés, *shops and accommodation than would normally be found in so small a town.* *Map, inside back cover*

▸▸ See also Sleeping p120, Eating and drinking p154, Sports p212

*The quickest way to get to Tofino from Vancouver is by float-plane from the International Airport Seaplane Terminal. Otherwise you can catch a ferry from Horseshoe Bay to Nanaimo, then a bus to Tofino. Tofino's busy Visitor Information Centre is at 121 3rd St, **T** 7253414, www.tofino-bc.com  Open Apr-Sep. A Pacific Rim National Park Pass costs $8 per day, $42 season pass.  See also p25*

#  Sights

## Clayoquot Sound and Barkley Sound

Tofino is in the middle of Clayoquot Sound, North America's largest surviving area of low-altitude temperate rainforest, one of the most biologically productive ecosystems on earth, and BC's first UN Biosphere Reserve (see box). It is, together with the Broken Islands Group of Barkley Sound to the south, one of the most outstanding spots for kayaking on the West Coast. The latter is an archipelago of over a hundred tiny scattered islands, difficult to reach and visited almost exclusively by kayakers. Coastal wilderness doesn't get much more remote than this, and the scenery is utterly pristine; there's a good chance of spotting marine wildlife, including major colonies of sealions. Not surprisingly, paddlers come here in droves, so don't expect to feel like a lone explorer. If anything, Clayoquot Sound is even more magnificent, though the islands are bigger and less numerous. It's less crowded with fellow kayakers, but more used by other vessels. Neither location is suitable for unaccompanied novices. Submerged rocks, reefs, sea caves, exposed channels, extreme, unpredicable weather, and freezing water lead to a few deaths every year.

## ★ Whale-watching and Hot Springs Cove

*Sea Trek Tours, T 7254412, www.seatrektours.bc.ca; Remote Passages, T 7253330, www.remotepassages.com; Ocean Outfitters, T 7252866, www.oceanoutfitters; Adventures Pacific, T 7252811, www.adventurespacific.com   Map inside back cover*

Every year some 24,000 grey whales migrate past Vancouver Island's West Coast on their way from Baja California to Siberia. The best time to see them is mid-March to early April, but you're practically guaranteed to see these and other whales throughout the summer, and this remains Tofino's number one excursion. Many companies, most of them long established and reputable, offer such trips. The main thing to decide before signing up is if you want to go in an inflatable zodiac or a hard-shelled boat. The former are faster, wetter and more exciting; the latter more suitable for pregnant women, and those with heart conditions or expensive cameras. Two reliable and recommended operators are *Sea Trek Tours*, who have a glass-bottomed boat and also run bear-watching tours, and *Remote Passages*, mainly zodiacs. Both companies offer tours that combine whale-watching with the 37-km trip to Hot Springs Cove, excellent value at roughly $90 for 6½ hours. The ride itself is a wonderful experience, taking you through some of the most pristine coastal scenery imaginable. From the jetty, a 2-km boardwalk leads through lush rainforest to the gloriously romantic springs. The water emerges at 43°C, then cascades down to the sea through a series of ever-cooler pools. Like most plum spots, it's understandably popular, so to avoid the summer crowds, think about paying a little more and staying over. Note that with the tourist hordes absent, clothing becomes more optional. *Ocean Outfitters* and *Adventures Pacific* will both leave you for a day or two as part of the tour package at no extra expense. Water taxis to the springs from Tofino cost about $60-70 return per person, or you could fly there with *Atleo Air or Tofino Airlines*.

## ★ Meares Island

*Rainforest Boatshuttle, **T** 7253793, and Meares Island Big Tree Taxi, **T** 7267848, both charge about $20 return.*

The lush rainforest of Meares Island is certainly a tempting sight from Tofino. Closest of the local big islands, just 15 minutes away by water taxi, this is one of the best places in Canada to walk among giant ancient trees, containing as it does one of the biggest remain- ing patches of virgin temperate rainforest in the world. On the 3-km loop of the **Big Cedar Trail** you'll see trees more than 6 m across and wonder why logging companies are still doing their best to cut them down. A shorter boardwalk stroll leads to the 2,000-year-old **Hanging Garden Cedar**, the biggest tree in Clayoquot Sound at 18.3 m in circumference.

## Flores Island

*Also easily reached by water taxi, about 20 km from Tofino.  Map, inside back cover*

Rarely is it possible to encounter Native Americans and their culture without feeling that either they or you are being exploited. But the village of Ahousat is a thriving First Nations community in the kind of unspoilt setting their ancestors enjoyed. The **Ahousat Wildside Heritage Trail** is a marvellous 11-km hike through rainforest and beaches to Mount Flores viewpoint. It's $20 to use unless staying at the *Hummingbird Hostel* in Ahousat, see Sleeping, p 121.

## Long Beach

*Parks Information Centre, mid-Jun-mid-Sep. Park fee $8 per day, $42 season pass.  Map, inside back cover*

The 130-km rollercoaster ride from Port Alberni provides a fitting introduction to the rugged West Coast. Most of the 36 km from Highway 4 to Tofino is occupied by Long Beach, the collective name for an almost unbroken series of forest-fringed bays and beaches, easily accessed from several points along the Pacific Rim Highway. Almost immediately on the right is the Parks Information Centre where you can pay the park fee and pick up a useful map which highlights possible trails in the area.

Given the pounding Pacific breakers and heavy rainfall hereabouts, this is not the place for sunbathing, but it's perfect for beachcombing and examining the rich wildlife of tide pools. The **surfing** is also about the best you'll find in Canada, but only for the experienced as the rip-tides can be deadly. A couple of places are recommended for gear, rentals, lessons and advice: *Storm Surf Shop*, 171 4th St, **T** 7252155. Lessons $59, rentals $25.

# Gulf Islands

The Strait of Georgia between Vancouver and Victoria is dotted with an archipelago of islands whose natural beauty and laid-back pace has attracted a rare blend of bohemians, hippies, eccentrics, draft-dodgers, pot-growers and an inordinate number of writers and artists. Together with arts and crafts, there is an emphasis on health and wholefoods, spirituality and healing, with an abundance of galleries and studios, spas and retreats, and weekend markets stocked with organic local produce. The islands provide a much better vantage point than Vancouver Island to appreciate the scenic beauty of this sheltered channel. The awesome Coast Mountains can be seen rising steeply behind convoluted coastlines and myriad islands of all shapes and sizes. Even the beaches tend to be better and less crowded than those on the main island, and marine life is as prevalent as elsewhere on the coast.

The Southern Gulf Islands are particularly clustered, making for excellent island-hopping, kayaking or sailing. Galiano and Salt Spring are the biggest, most easily reached and offer the most diversions. Unfortunately, they are also the busiest, especially at the height of summer, when accommodation can get very tight.

*BC Ferries run to the Gulf Islands from Vancouver's Tsawwassan and Victoria's Swartz Bay. The most reliable way of getting around these islands is by bike or kayak, which both allow access to parts other travellers cannot reach. Hitchhiking is a way of life here; if a car doesn't stop for you, it's usually a tourist.*

# Galiano Island

*Despite its popularity and proximity to Vancouver, Galiano is still nicely undeveloped, the closest thing even to a village being the ferry terminal of **Sturdies Bay**. There are plenty of walks through old-growth forest, much of it protected by the assiduous efforts of locals, and places to swim. There are no banks or cash machines, so bring sufficient cash. Nor is there a tourist office, just a booth with ads and leaflets.* Map, inside back cover

*Galiano Island Visitors' Association, **T** 5392233, www.galianoisland. com  Issues a free map for multiple beach access points. Galiano Bicycle Rental, 36 Burrill Rd, Sturdies Bay, **T** 5399906. Galiano Boat Rentals, Montague Harbour, **T** 5399828. Kayak rental and tours from Galiano Island Sea Kayaking, 637 Southwind Drive, **T** 1888-5392930, www.galianoislandsea kayaking.com  Sporades Tours Inc, **T** 5392278. Sightseeing on a fishing vessel. Captain has 40 years' experience.*

## ◉ Sights

The long, skinny finger of Galiano sits in the Georgia Strait pointing northwest away from Sturdies Bay in the southeast. Sturdies Bay Road connects fairly soon with Porlier Pass Road, which runs the length of the island. Alternatively, just after the ferry, a left turn down Burrill takes you along Bluff Road and through Bluffs Park, a beautiful chunk of old-growth forest. Shortly thereafter, a left fork leads to Active Pass Drive, and the trailhead for ascending **Mount Galiano**, a satisfying hike leading to views of the Olympic

Mountains, Navy Channel and, on a clear day, all of the Southern Gulf Islands. If you take the right fork, a left down Montague Road eventually connects back with Porlier Pass Road, just before **Montague Harbour Provincial Marine Park**. There are three white shell beaches here, a café and store, wonderful sunsets, and a great campground. A 3-km shoreline trail runs around Gray Peninsula. Two-thirds along the island, Cottage Way gives access to **Bodega Ridge**, a 3-km walk with views all along. **Dionisio Point Provincial Park** at the west end has camping, with many rare flowers and fine views, but marine access only. You can dive there with **Galiano Diving**, T 5393109, www.galianodiving.com, who also operate a water taxi.

## Salt Spring Island

*Salt Spring has three different harbours. Swartz Bay ferries arrive at* **Fulford Bay** *in the south, $6 return, 25.25 with vehicle; Tsawwassen ferries arrive at* **Long Harbour**, *$9, $44.50 with vehicle on the outward journey, $5, $23.25 returning. Harbour Air Seaplanes, T 5375525, www.harbourair.com, have regular daily flights from Vancouver, $65 one way.* **Ganges** *is at the northern end of the island, some 15 km on the main Fulford-Ganges Rd from Fulford Bay, about 6 km from the other harbours. Bikes and scooters can be rented at the hostel. Bikes and kayaks can be rented at Saltspring Kayaking, 2923 Fulford- Ganges Rd, T 6534222. Otherwise there's Silver Shadow Taxi, T 5373030. Visitor Information Centre, by the shopping centre car park, 121 Lower Ganges Rd, Ganges, T 5375252. Daily 0900-1600. Also visit www.saltspringtoday.bc.ca  Map, inside back cover*

## ◉ Sights

Salt Spring is the busiest, biggest and most populated of the Gulf Islands, and the only one with a settlement that could be considered a town, the oddly named Ganges. There are more eating and drinking options here than usual, and more chance of finding walk-in accommodation at any time of year. The pay-off is the loss of tranquility and quaintness, though these are easily found elsewhere on this sheep-dotted island. For local crafts and organic produce, cheeses and conserves, music and food, head for the excellent **Saturday Market**, *0830-1530 Apr-Oct*, in Centennial Park, Ganges, www.saltspringmarket.com

At the south end of the island, 9 km east of Fulford Harbour and at the end of Beaver Point Road, is Ruckle Provincial Park, the largest and one of the nicest on the Gulf Islands. Trails here incorporate forest, 7 km of shoreline and farmland containing historic buildings. There's a good chance of spotting marine life and birds, but the park's outstanding feature is its campground (see Sleeping, p125). For some truly awe-inspiring vistas, head to the top of **Mount Maxwell Provincial Park**. There are some trails past big old trees, but the temptation is just to sit down and gawp. It's also a good place to experience the full power of the winds that can whistle down the strait. Just south of Ganges, take Cranberry Road west to Mount Maxwell Road, then it's a stiff climb for 8 km.

Longer, more remote hikes lead up Mount Tuam and Mount Bruce, west of Fulford Bay. Swimming is good at Vesuvius Bay or at St Mary Lake (north of Ganges) and Cusheon Lake (south) for fresh water. For sailing, kayaking, biking, hiking and climbing, see Sports, p124.

There are many art stores and studios in Ganges, most offering the chance to meet the artist. Ask at the Information Centre for a full list. **Art Craft**, held from June-September in Ganges' Mahon Hall, provides a great opportunity to see (and buy) the work of some 200 or so Gulf Island artists. The **July Festival of the Arts**, **T** 5374167, is a month-long orgy of what the Gulf Islands do best. **Coastal Currents Gallery**, on Hereford Avenue, has an exceptionally tasteful selection of arts, crafts and gifts well arranged in a big house. **Vortex Gallery**, Grace Point Square, www.vortexgallery.com, displays the work of local artists who have made names for themselves in the international art world. Whilst this is a commercial gallery, and therefore free, the prices are so elevated that nobody expects visitors to do much more than browse. **ArtSpring**, 100 Jackson, **T** 5372102, www.artspring.ca, is the island's main venue for music and performing arts.

Most of the expensive hotels are Downtown and along Robson Street and there are some good mid-range options in the heart of town, too, as well as most of the city's excellent selection of hostels. It's possible to find a perfectly decent double room in a hotel for considerably less than $100. B&Bs, a more personal, often better-value alternative, tend to be in attractive, quiet neighbourhoods like the West End, Kitsilano, North Shore, or Mount Pleasant, a well-to-do residential area in South Vancouver. If you're on a budget, the hostels really are first class, but the better ones do fill up fast in summer. Both of Vancouver's universities offer cheap, long-stay accommodation in summer. To find an apartment, the best resource is the classified section of the *Vancouver Sun*. Campsites are a poor option, far from town, and often only take RVs. Arriving in Vancouver without a reservation is not usually a problem. The Visitor Information Centre is the best place to turn for help.

$ **Sleeping codes**

| | | | |
|---|---|---|---|
| LL | $280 and over | C | $75-100 |
| L | $220-280 | D | $50-75 |
| AL | $180-220 | E | $25-50 |
| A | $140-180 | F | $25 and under |
| B | $100-140 | | |

Price

Prices are for a double room in high season.

# Downtown and Yaletown

### Hotels

**LL Fairmont Waterfront**, 900 Canada Place Way, **T** 6911991, www.thewaterfronthotel.com  *Map 3, C2, p248*  About the least stuffy and most comfortable of the big, waterfront hotels. Rooms are simple and compact, but tastefully decorated, and most offer views of the harbour and North Shore mountain. Staff are helpful and attentive. Facilities include a heated outdoor pool, exercise room, steam rooms, hot tub and a terrace with great views.

**LL The Landis Hotel and Suites**, 1200 Hornby St, **T** 6813555, www.landissuitesvancouver.com  *Map 2, G6, p251*  If facilities and value for money are your priorities, this is the place. These vast two-bedroom suites come with fully equipped kitchens, patio-style dining rooms, big living rooms and simple but pleasant decor. Those on higher floors offer good city views. Facilities include an indoor pool, hot tub and exercise room.  Continental breakfast included. Parking available. A great option for two couples or a family.

**LL Opus**, 322 Davie St, Yaletown, **T** 6426787, www.opushotel.com *Map 2, H8, p251*  Brand new in 2002, this impossibly hip boutique hotel was designed to mirror Yaletown's upmarket urban chic. Rooms and suites follow five unique designs with art, furnishings and amenities conspiring to create specific atmospheres from minimalist to retro to post-modern eclectic. Even the mirrors, wash basins and elevator are impressive. Facilities include a fitness room, a French brasserie with outdoor seating, a Zen garden courtyard and parking.

LL **Sheraton Suites Le Soleil**, 567 Hornby St, **T** 6323000, www.lesoleilhotel.com *Map 3, D1, p252* If money is no object and you want to be treated like royalty, this is the place. Every aspect of this hotel has been custom made to the highest standards with the emphasis on old-world luxury. Service is bend-over-backwards impeccable. Facilities include an indoor pool, fitness room, sauna and a fine restaurant that's as opulent as the hotel.

LL-L **Sheraton Vancouver Wall Centre Hotel**, 1088 Burrard St, **T** 3311000, www.sheratonvancouver.com *Map 2, F7, p250* Housed in the city's two tallest buildings, this sleek hotel is as aesthetically pleasing as it is modern. Rooms are a reasonable size, comfy and pleasant, with floor-to-ceiling windows making the most of incredible city views. Facilities include an indoor pool and hot tub. The restaurant, *Indigo*, is an upbeat, funky place.

AL **The Meridian at 910 Beach**, 910 Beach Av, **T** 6095100, www.910beach.com *Map 2, H4, p251* Pleasantly located on False Creek, *The Meridian* has studios and a variety of attractive, open-plan, fully equipped suites, some with patio or balcony. Floor-to-ceiling windows give views of the water, Granville Market or the city. There's a fitness centre, and continental breakfast is included in the price.

A **The Inn at False Creek**, 1135 Howe St, **T** 6820229, www.qualityhotel.ca *Map 2, G7, p251* This is the best of a cluster of hotels in an uninspiring, but conveniently central, location. Rooms are well equipped and reasonably sized. Nothing special, but good value. Extras include an outdoor pool and free passes to *Fitness World* a block away.

A-B **Marriott Residence Inn**, 1234 Hornby St, **T** 6881234, www.residenceinn.com *Map 2, G6, p251* The *Marriot*'s one-room suites come with big beds and windows, a sitting area and kitchenette. Extras include a small gym, indoor pool and sauna, and a free continental breakfast buffet. A great deal for the price.

B **Sandman Inn**, 180 W Georgia, **T** 6812211, www.sandmanhotels.com *Map 3, G2, p253* The rooms here are clean and functional, the location is central, the price reasonable and facilities include an indoor pool, health club, hot tub and parking. Some one- and two-bed suites also. Lounge, bar and grill downstairs.

B-D **Victorian Hotel**, 514 Homer, **T** 6816369, www.victorian-hotel.com *Map 3, E3, p252* The *Victorian*'s rooms are small and some share a bathroom, but the comfort, decor and ambience are far beyond anything else in this price range. Hardwood floors, good art, pastel shades and tasteful bathrooms, together with the friendly, attentive service, give an impression of luxury at budget prices. Continental breakfast included. Reservations recommended.

C **Comfort Inn Downtown**, 654 Nelson St, **T** 6054333, www.comfortinndowntown.com *Map 2, G8, p251* Certainly the best deal in its range, this long-standing hotel has just been totally renovated in a hip retro 50s style, with lots of black and white photos and neon signs. A continental breakfast and nightlife pass are included, but the real bonus is the central location and great price.

## Hostels

**D-E  HI Vancouver Central**, 1025 Granville St, **T** 6855335.
*Map 2, G7, p250*  A brand new and very central hostel. Dorms and private rooms. Common room, express kitchen (microwaves, no stove), shared bath, lockers, trips arranged.

**D-E  Global Village Backpackers**, 1018 Granville St, **T** 6828226.  *Map 2, G8, p251*  This excellent hostel is centrally located in a funky, colourful building, with young, friendly staff. Dorms and private doubles, some with en suite baths. There's a spacious common room with lots of sofas, a pool table, licensed café and internet. Facilities include a big kitchen, laundry, lockers/storage room, a TV room with free movies and a travel desk to book tours. Patio for smokers. Pub crawls five days a week. Will be serving cheap breakfast.

**E  The Cambie Hostel Seymour**, 515 Seymour St, **T** 6847757.
*Map 3, E2, p252*  Situated in a quieter location than its equally popular and well-run sister hotel (in Gastown), this one has small, two-bed rooms or private doubles, but no dorms, and so tends to have less of a backpacker-style atmosphere. There's a small kitchen, a common room, laundry facilities, coin-op and storage (but no lockers). Various ski/ice-hockey packages are offered.

# Gastown, East Side and Chinatown

## Hotels

**D  Patricia Hotel**, 403 E Hastings, **T** 2554301.  *Map 3, F7, p252*
The best budget option in town, housed in a nicely renovated 1914 building enlivened with many plants, and surprisingly classy given the seedy area. Rooms are simple, clean and comfy, with en suite

baths. Some even have fine views. Price includes a huge breakfast at a café down the street. Smoking on every floor but the fifth, weekly rates off season. Helpful staff on duty 24 hours.

## Hostels

**E  The Cambie Hostel Gastown**, 300 Cambie St, **T** 6846466, www.cambiehostels.com *Map 3, E3, p252*  Well-run and handily situated, this popular backpacker hostel has 142 beds, mostly in dorms. Its common rooms are a good place to meet travellers and pick up  information. Free breakfast (coffee and muffin), no kitchen, but the popular, down-to-earth pub downstairs has a cheap restaurant, and there's an excellent bakery next door.

# West End and Stanley Park

## Hotels

**LL-L  Listel Vancouver**, 1300 Robson St, **T** 6848461, www.listel-vancouver.com *Map 2, C6, p250*  This purpose-built hotel is impressively beautiful and stylish throughout. Rooms are thoughtfully equipped with big windows and TVs. 'Museum rooms' are decorated with First Nations art and exquisite hand-carved furnishings. 'Gallery rooms' were each uniquely conceived by different designers and feature chaise longues by the windows. Facilities include a fitness centre and hot tub. Service is personal and attentive. Highly recommended.

**AL  Pacific Palisades**, 1277 Robson St, **T** 6880461, www.pacificpalisadeshotel.com *Map 2, C6, p250*  The decor throughout this hotel is bright, playful and mildly psychedelic, with vibrant greens and yellows, stripes and spots, and plenty of funky pieces of art. Rooms are big and comfortable with first-rate furnishings. The facilities – indoor pool, health club, sauna and whirlpool – are about the best in town. Free wine-tasting from 1700-1800. Suites with a balcony are more expensive but sleep four. Highly recommended. *Zin Restaurant* shares the hotel's sense of colour, style and eclecticism.

**AL Rosellen Suites at Stanley Park**, 2030 Barclay St, **T** 6894807, www.rosellensuites.com *Map 2, A3, p250* Nicely situated right next to the park, the *Rosellen* has spacious and fully equipped one- and two-bedroom suites that can sleep up to six ($15 extra per person). All have kitchens and extras like stereos. Some have fireplaces. Parking and membership at a nearby health club and the Aquatic Centre are included.

**A Blue Horizon Hotel**, 1225 Robson St, **T** 6884461, www.bluehorizonhotel.com *Map 2, C6, p250* One of a handful of mid-range options grouped together on Robson St. Rooms here are plain, but large and well equipped, with balconies and good views on two sides. Those with two beds ($10 more) sleep four and are much bigger. Facilities include a small pool, hot tub, sauna and fitness centre. Very good value.

**A Oceanside Apartment Hotel**, 1847 Pendrell St, **T** 6825641, www.oceanside-hotel.com *Map 2, C3, p250* Pleasant, fairly spacious suites with small kitchens, ideal for two couples. Its main advantage is the location on a very quiet West End street close to Stanley Park and Denman Street. Good value.

**B Tropicana Motor Inn**, 1361 Robson St, **T** 6875724. *Map 2, C6, p250* Best value of the hotels clustered on Robson St. The suites suffer from unaesthetic decor, but are a reasonable size, with small kitchens and high-quality TVs. Higher floors offer good views over the metropolis. Facilities include indoor swimming pool, sauna and parking. Can sleep four ($10 extra per person).

B-C **Sylvia Hotel**, 1154 Gilford St, **T** 6819321, www.sylviahotel.com
*Map 2, C2, p250*   This landmark vine-covered building has been open continuously since 1912 and was the tallest in the West End until the mid-50s. The slightly faded rooms are nothing special, though some offer views of Stanley Park next door. Heavily booked due to price and location. Suites are more expensive but are much bigger, have kitchenettes and can sleep four ($15 extra per person).

## B&Bs

A   **English Bay Inn B&B**, 1968 Comox St, **T** 6838002, www.englishbayinn.com *Map 2, B3, p250*   This lovely 1930s Tudor-style house is lavishly furnished with antiques, rugs and a grandfather clock, with a pretty garden at the back. The six en suite rooms are quite small and twee, but attractive and comfortable.

A-B   **O Canada House B&B**, 1114 Barclay St, **T** 6880555, www.ocanadahouse.com *Map 2, E6, p250*   This 1897 Queen Anne house, sumptuously decorated with period antiques, was once home to the man who wrote the lyrics of Canada's national anthem. There's a wrap-around porch, English garden, and sherry in the front parlour in the evenings. The seven en suite rooms, some with fireplaces, are smallish, but suitably luxurious.

## Hostels

D-E   **HI Vancouver Downtown**, 1114 Burnaby St, **T** 6844565, www.hihostels.ca *Map 2, F5, p250*   This clean and professional hostel offers four-bed dorms and simple private rooms with shared bath. Top-notch facilities include a TV room, library, games room with pool table, laundry, lockers, storage room, dining room and large kitchen. Many cheap activities arranged, such as tours, kayaking and club nights. Convenient but quiet, free shuttle to/from the bus and train stations. Reservations recommended.

# Granville Island and Vanier Park

## Hotels

**LL-AL Granville Island Hotel**, 1253 Johnstone St, **T** 6837373, www.granvilleislandhotel.com *Map 2, K5, p251* The varied rooms here are decent enough and some have balconies, but the price reflects the prime location rather than the no-better-than-average decor and furnishings. Facilities include a glassed-in hot tub, steam room and a very pleasant lounge and restaurant.

# Kitsilano and Point Grey

## B&Bs

**A Camelot Inn**, 2212 Larch St, **T** 7396941, www.camelotinn vancouver.com *Map 5, D5, p255* A beautifully restored 1912 house with hardwood floors, Persian rugs and decor that for once is not excessive. The four en suite rooms are just as tasteful and reasonably sized. Breakfast included.

**B Mickey's Kits Beach Chalet**, 2146 1st Av, **T** 7393342 *Close to Kits Beach. Map 5, C6, p255* Six pleasant, bright and refreshingly no-nonsense rooms, four with en suite, two with balconies. On a quiet road, with a friendly and helpful host. Breakfast included.

**C Between Friends**, 1916 Arbutus, **T** 7345082. *Map 5, C6, p255* Three small but agreeable rooms in a house close to the most interesting part of 4th Avenue, but still within walking distance of the beach and park. Only one room has en suite bath, but the nicest has a balcony and skylight. Pleasant sitting room and a very affable hostess.

C **Graeme's House**, 2735 Waterloo St, **T** 7321488, www.graeme webster.com *Close to the most happening section of Broadway.* *Map 5, E2, p255* A pretty heritage house with lots of interesting decorative features, plus private decks, a rear flower-decked patio and beautiful gardens. Somewhat let down by the rooms which are a bit small and twee. Continental breakfast included. Friendly and knowledgeable hosts.

B **Maple House**, 1533 Maple St, **T** 7395833, www.maplehouse.com *Close to Kits Beach and Vanier Park.* *Map 5, B7, p255* Fairly nice en suite rooms in an attractive 1900 home, whose best selling point is its location close to Kits Beach and Vanier Park. Full breakfast incuded.

## Hostels and university campuses

B-D **University of BC**, 5961 Student Union Blvd, **T** 8221000, www.ubcconferences.com *May-Aug Map 1, G1, p249* During the summer the university offers a broad variety of long-stay options, from basic one-bed rooms with shared bath, kitchen and common room, to fully equipped suites.

D-E **HI Jericho Beach Hostel**, 1515 Discovery St, **T** 2243208, www.hihostels.ca *A free shuttle runs to and from the Downtown HI Hostel and bus station 7 times per day 0700-1345 in winter, 0800-1600 in summer with an extra 4 from 1800-2200. Take bus No 4 (UBC). Map 1, G1, p249* Built in the 1930s as a barracks, this vast and interesting building is now the largest hostel in Canada, with 288 dorm beds and 10 private rooms, all with shared bath. Very long dorms are divided up into four-bed alcoves. To avoid bed bugs, sleeping bags are prohibited. All the usual top-notch facilities are here: a massive kitchen and dining room, TV room, games room with pool table, library, laundry, big lockers, storage room, bike rental for $20 per day. Open 24 hours, with an information desk in summer. Free or cheap tours and hikes, even activities like sailing. The main factor here is the location, a beautiful and quiet spot right on the beach, but a long way from town.

# South and East Vancouver

## Hotels and motels

**AL-A Fairmont Vancouver Airport**, T 2075200, www.fairmont.com *In the airport Map 1, I3, p249* It doesn't get much more convenient than this, situated right in the main airport building, this luxury hotel offers large, soundproof rooms, attentive service and facilities such as an indoor pool, hot tub and spa.

**B Delta Vancouver Airport**, 3500 Cessna Dr, T 2781241, www.deltavancouverairport.com *Close to the airport. Map 1, I3, p249* The nicest place to stay close to the airport, thanks to its riverside location surrounded by dozens of scenic little boats, with a pub (the *Elephant and Castle*) housed in a small pagoda on the water. Facilities include an outdoor pool, exercise room, restaurant and airport pick-up.

**B Holiday Inn Express**, 9351 Bridgeport Rd, T 4654329, www.hi-express.bc.ca *Map 1, I4, p249* The best value of several mid-price places huddled together close to the airport. Those without a reservation should shop around as there are often bargains to be found. Rooms are ordinary but pleasant. Continental breakfast and airport shuttle included.

**D City Centre Motor Hotel**, 2111 Main St, T 8767166. *Map 6, 7A, p256* This is the kind of standard motel more readily found further out. The predictably plain rooms have en suite baths and TV. The advantages are the price, its proximity to the Science World SkyTrain and an interesting part of Main Street, and the ease with which you can reach Downtown.

## Guesthouses and B&B

B **Columbia Cottage B&B**, 205 W 14th Av, Mount Pleasant, **T** 8745327. *Map 6, B5, p256* A pretty house on a quiet, residential; street, with an art deco living room for guests and pleasant gardens. The five en suite rooms are small but attractive. Full vegetarian breakfast included. Helpful owner doesn't live on site.

B **Douglas Guest House**, 456 W 13th Av, Mount Pleasant, **T** 8723060, www.dougwin.com *Map 6, B5, p256* The best of three similar B&Bs owned by the same people. Eight fairly large rooms/suites, with en suite in all but two, and TVs. The decor is simple but elegant throughout, with a small common room and a glassed-in sun room with patio that also serves as dining room.

## Camping

E-F **Burnaby Caribou RV Park**, 8765 Caribou Pl, **T** 4201722. *About 16 km from Downtown. Bus No 101, and close to the useful 99 route. Map 1, H7, p249* Probably the most salubrious campground, and closer than most. Lots of facilities including heated indoor pool, hot tub, exercise room and games room.

E -F **Peace Arch RV Park**, 14601 40th Av, T 5947009, www.peacearchrvpark.com *About 28 km southeast of Vancouver.* Large campground with hook-ups, tent sites, outdoor swimming pool and games room. Suitable if you want to stop on your way to or from the US border.

# North Shore

## Hotels and motels

**B Grouse Inn**, 1633 Capilano Rd, **T** 9887101, www.grouseinn.com
*Map 1, F4, p248* The best value of several standard motels around
the busy Capilano/Marine Drive intersection. Convenient but noisy.
Rooms are nothing special. Continental breakfast included,
outdoor pool, free parking.

**C-D Travelodge Lions Gate**, 2060 Marine Dr, **T** 9855311,
www.lionsgatetravelodge.com *Map 1, F3, p248* Standard chain
motel with an outdoor pool. Selling points are the convenient, if
noisy, location and the very reasonable price.

## B&Bs

**L-A Beach Side**, 4208 Evergreen Av, West Vancouver, **T** 9227773,
www.beach.bc.ca *Map 1, F2, p248* This extremely stylish house is
gloriously located right on the beach close to Lighthouse Park. Its
three luxurious en suite rooms/suites have TV and VCR and some
have their own jacuzzi, views, garden patio, kitchen or fireplace.

**L-A Crystal's View**, 420 Temple Cres, **T** 9873952, www.bc-bed
andbreakfast.com *Map 1, E5, p248* Large, sumptuously decorated
en suite rooms, some with jacuzzi and balcony, in a very attractive
house. Guest sitting room and patio with winning views of the city,
but not the most convenient location.

**L-A Thistledown House**, 3910 Capilano Rd, **T** 9867173,
www.thistle-down.com *Map 1, E4, p248* Situated between
Capilano Canyon and Grouse Mountain, this warm and attractive
1920s heritage home is tastefully decorated and set in gardens.

## Mount Pleasant's pillow stops

*Vancouver's B&Bs, more personal and often better value than hotels, tend to be in the city's genteel, residential areas.*

Five pleasant en suite rooms. Deck, guest lounge and full breakfast included.

**AL-A  Queen Anne Manor**, 4606 Wickenden Rd, Deep Cove, **T** 9293239, www.n-vancouver.com  *Map 1, F7, p248*  A gorgeous, turreted, Victorian-style home, sumptuously decorated and furnished. Two guest sitting rooms, one with TV, one with library. The two rooms and one suite are a bit twee for some tastes.

**A-B  A Gazebo in the Garden**, 310 St James Rd E, **T** 9833331, www.agazebointhegarden.com  *Map 1, E6, p248*  Beautiful prairie-style heritage home decorated with antiques and set in a stunning garden. Four comfortable en suite rooms with TVs. Full breakfast.

**B-C Mountainside Manor**, 5909 Nancy Greene Way, **T** 9909772, www.vancouver-bc.com/MountainsideManor *Map 1, D4, p248* Unusual, elegant home en route to Grouse Mountain, most suitable if you've got a vehicle. Light and airy interior with guest lounge, large deck and a lovely garden. Four pleasant rooms with en suite or private bath.

## Camping

**F-E Capilano RV Park**, 295 Tomahawk Av, **T** 9874722 *Near Lion's Gate Bridge on North Shore. Map 1, F3, p248* An unattractive campground, more like a parking lot, but easily the best located. Facilities include full hook-ups, pool, jacuzzi, playground and games room.

# Squamish and Garibaldi Provincial Park

### Hotels and hostels

**B Howe Sound Inn and Brewing Company**, 37801 Cleveland Av, **T** 8922603, www.howesound.com Undoubtedly *the* place to stay in Squamish. An uncharacteristically handsome building whose simple and stylish rooms have wooden furniture and mountain views. Facilities include sauna, granite climbing wall and a great brew-pub and restaurant with views of Stawamus Chief from the patio.

**C Sunwolf Outdoor Centre**, 70002 Squamish Valley Rd, Brackendale, **T** 8981537, www.sunwolf.net *4 km off Highway 99.* Ten pretty and modern cabins with fir floors, pine furniture and gas fires. Situated in 2 ha of grounds at the confluence of two rivers, with a volleyball court and firepits. Eagle-watching, whitewater rafting and kayaking arranged. Onsite café.

**D-E Squamish Hostel**, 38490 Buckley Av, **T** 8929240. In summer 2003, this rather shabby hostel will be replaced by a brand new, large and attractive one on the highway at the entrance to town. Accommodation is in 4-6-bed dorms or private rooms with en suite bath. Facilities include a lounge with fireplace, a large kitchen and dining room, TV room showing films, a games room, laundry and drying room, lockers and storage, a balcony with views of the Chief, internet access, BBQ and a bouldering cave.

## Camping

**F Alice Lake Provincial Park**, **T** 8983678. *13 km north of Squamish.* 108 treed, private sites, none very close to the beach, 12 are walk-in only. Pretty lake with fishing and swimming, hot showers and a big grassy area.

**F Klahanie Campground**, **T** 8923435. *5 mins south of town, opposite Shannon Falls.* Fairly private sites with plenty of trees, full hook-ups, showers and a restaurant.

# Whistler

## Hotels and hostels

**LL Canadian Pacific Château Whistler Resort**, 4599 Château Blvd, **T** 9388000, www.chateauwhistlerresort.com *At the base of Blackcomb Mountain.* One of a chain of hotels built by the railway and reminiscent of a French château. As grandiose as they come, with impeccable service, and facilities such as pool, hot tub, gym and a handful of restaurants. Will arrange any kind of activity. There's a full spa on site and a golf course next door (neither included in price, but ask about packages).

**AL  Listel Hotel**, 4121 Village Green, **T** 9321133, www.listelhotel.com  Whistler is full of expensive hotels that lack character. This one is more stylish than most, but rooms are still rather small and nothing special. Facilities include an outdoor heated pool, saunas, jacuzzi and a fine bistro/lounge.

**A  Edgewater Lodge**, 8841 Highway 99, Meadow Pk, **T** 9320688, www.edgewater-lodge.com  For those with their own transport, this is the place. Situated on a small peninsula jutting out into Green Lake, it's a very beautiful and quiet spot, with lake and mountain views from every room. The 18 forested hectares also have plenty of trails for walking, biking and skiing. There's an outdoor jacuzzi and a gorgeous lakefront dining room renowned for its European cuisine and service.

**C-E  The Shoestring Lodge**, 7124 Nancy Greene Dr, Village North, **T** 9323338.  A great budget choice, new and clean, with common room and kitchen. All four-person dorms and private rooms have en suite bathroom. Conveniently close to town, with its own pub and restaurant.

**E  HI Whistler**, 5678 Alta Lake Rd, **T** 9325492  *Opposite side of lake. 5 buses into town per day.*  The budget option of choice, in a lovely lakeside setting. Clean, quiet and very friendly. Mostly dorms with some private rooms. Facilities include common room and kitchen, sauna and internet with canoes and bikes available to borrow. Reservations essential.

## B&Bs

**A  Cedar Springs B&B**, 8106 Cedar Springs Rd, Alpine Meadows, **T** 9388007, www.whistlerbb.com  *4 km north of Whistler village.* A superior B&B in a quiet semi-rural setting with eight attractive rooms of a very varied nature, all decorated in wood. Communal lounge with fire, balconies, hot tub, sauna, videos and bike rental. Three-course breakfast, afternoon tea and a shuttle to the hill are all included.

**B Edelweiss Pension**, 7162 Nancy Greene Dr, Village North, **T** 9323641. Eight comfortable en suite rooms, some with balconies and views. Extras include a guest lounge with fireplace, whirlpool, sauna, patios, garden and a full cooked breakfast. Great value.

## Camping

**E Riverside RV Resort**, 8018 Mons Rd, **T** 9055533. *About 1.5 km from the village off Blackcomb Way.* Situated on 16 ha by a creek , this is about the only real choice for campers and open year round. Treed, fairly private sights for tents, full service for RVs, and attractive, fully equipped log cabins with kitchen, VCR and small patios (AL). Facilities include hot showers, BBQ, laundry, games room with pool table, café, a handy grocery store, volleyball court and putting course. They rent bikes, skis and other gear, arrange tours, and provide free shuttles to the gondolas.

# Victoria

### Hotels and motels

**LL-L The Fairmont Empress**, 721 Government St, **T** 3848111, www.fairmont.com  If you want to feel like royalty and expense is no issue, this is the place. The most striking and sumptuous building in town, overflowing with chandeliers, marble and exquisite antique furnishings. There are several upmarket restaurants and genteel tearooms, plus a full health club and spa (not included in price). Impeccable service, mostly enjoyed by Japanese tourists. Ask for a room with harbour view.

**LL-B  Dashwood Manor**, 1 Cook St, T 3855517, www.dashwoodmanor.com  This huge, old, waterfront house has a broad variety of elegant Victorian rooms, all with en suite baths and kitchens, some with balcony, jacuzzi or ocean views. The cheaper ones are excellent value. Breakfast and evening cheese and wine are included.

**L  The Magnolia**, 623 Courtenay St, T 3810999, www.magnoliahotel.com  Slightly more modest than the *Empress*, but still extremely plush, as the gold-leaf, barrel-vaulted ceiling, alabaster chandeliers and mahogany panelling in the lobby will confirm. Rooms are comfy, tasteful and well equipped, with floor-to-ceiling windows. Continental breakfast is included, but the full-service spa is not (ask about packages).

**L-A  Holland House Inn**, 595 Michigan St, T 3846644. Seventeen rooms in a large, very attractive old house in the quiet residential zone between harbour and ocean. All have balconies, some have a fireplace and four-poster bed. Full breakfast included.

★ **L-A  Swans Suite Hotel**, 506 Pandora Av, T 3613310, www.swanshotel.com  For genuine style without the pomp, this is the one. No rooms, just huge, gorgeous, fully equipped suites built of brick and wood with high ceilings and full of great art. Downstairs is a superb brew-pub and restaurant, with one of the best Native art collections anywhere. Excellent value and highly recommended.

**B-C  Admiral Motel**, 257 Belleville St, T 3886267, www.admiral.bc.ca  The most reasonably priced and probably the friendliest of many hotels along the Inner Harbour. Rooms are nothing special, but each has a balcony or patio. Suites also available, as is parking. Continental breakfast included. Their website is a useful source of information.

C **Bedford Regency**, 1140 Government St, **T** 3846835. This deceptively fancy building harbours a range of smallish, fairly standard rooms, some with jacuzzi tubs. The cheaper ones are good value, especially given the central location.

D **Daffodil Inn**, 680 Garbally Rd, **T** 3868351. *Fairly close to town.* The best of the super-cheap motels, with big rooms and kitchenettes taking the edge off the dated decor and ugly carpets.

## B&Bs

L-A **Spinnakers Guesthouse**, 308 Catherine St, **T** 3842739. Beautiful and spacious B&B-style rooms in an 1884 heritage home, or modern garden suites in a Mediterranean-style building, all with en suite baths and private entrance. Breakfast included. Wonderful and popular brew-pub/restaurant on premises.

B **Birdcage Walk Guest House**, 505 Government St, **T** 3890804. One of the nicest of Victoria's many heritage homes converted into B&Bs. All rooms are a decent size with tasteful decor, en suite baths and kitchens. Handy location close to the harbour. Breakfast is inlcuded in the price.

## Hostels

E **Hostelling International Victoria**, 516 Yates St, **T** 3853232, victoria@hihostels.bc.ca   Quiet, well-run hostel in a nice big building with high ceilings, conveniently located in the heart of Downtown. Facilities include a common room, big kitchen, laundry and lockers. Private rooms are available for a few dollars more.

E **Ocean Island Backpackers Inn**, 791 Pandora Av, **T** 3851788, www.oceanisland.com   A more rough and ready place, geared towards young travellers, with pub crawls and the like arranged.

Also enjoys a fairly central location. Shared common room, café and kitchen. Dorms and private rooms available.

## Camping

**F  McDonald Provincial Park**, McDonald Park Rd, **T** 3912300  *Off Highway 17 near Swartz Bay.*  Forty-nine attractive treed sites, but only convenient for those catching a late ferry in or early ferry out.

**F  Thetis Lake**, 1938 W Park Lane, **T** 4783845.  *10 km from Victoria*. The closest campground to town, with a pleasant lakeside location with a beach and good swimming.  Hot showers and laundry.

# Tofino and around

## Hotels and resorts

**LL  Wickaninnish Inn**, Osprey Lane, Chesterman Beach, **T** 7253100, www.wickinn.com  The swankiest option. Rooms have natural, stylish decor with lots of wood, including handmade driftwood furniture. Balconies and floor-to-ceiling windows make the most of ocean views, which are exceptional even by West Coast standards. Lots of extras such as fireplaces, CD players, books, binoculars, huge TVs and oversized tubs. Their *Pointe Restaurant* is renowned as one of the best in the west. Full spa not included in price, but ask about packages.

**LL-AL  Pacific Sands Beach Resort**, 1421 Pacific Rim Highway, Chesterman Beach, **T** 7253322, www.pacificsands.com  With ample lawns, hiking trails and its own stretch of manicured beach, this is another lovely spot. Attractive one- and two-bedroom suites with decks, kitchens and fireplaces, or two-bedroom cottages with all mod cons.

**LL-B  Middle Beach Lodge**, 400 Mackenzie Beach, **T** 7252900, www.middlebeach.com  *3 km south of Tofino*. There are plenty of all-inclusive resorts in Tofino but, set in 16 ha of of oceanfront grounds and with its own beach, this is one of the best. The timber lodge features hardwood floors, pine furnishings and stone fireplaces. Lodge rooms are quite plain but have decks with views. There are aso some suites and luxurious oceanfront cabins. Continental breakfast included, dinner available.

**AL  Innchanter**, Hot Springs Cove, **T** 6701149, www.innchanter.com  This 1920s arts-and-crafts-style coastal freighter, moored just off the dock, offers the Cove's most intimate and stylish accommodation. The five rooms are small but cute and full of character, with shared bath. The shared living room has a fireplace, sofas and a splendid library. The price includes breakfast and dinner, excellent food often involving locally caught seafood. Recommended.

**B  Hot Springs Lodge**, Hot Springs Cove, **T** 6701106. A motel-style set-up with kitchenettes in the ensuite rooms. Guests are advised to bring groceries. Situated across from the water from the Springs, they lend row boats at no extra charge.

**F  Maquinna Campground**, **T** 6701100. This small native-run campground is beautifully situated in a forest right on the ocean, next to the dock and close to the Springs. There are no facilities other than drinking water, wood and firepits.

**E  Hummingbird Hostel**, Ahousat, Meares Island, **T** 6709679, A small and friendly native-run hostel. Beds are in dorms, with shared bathrooms, common room and kitchen facilities.

## B&Bs

**AL-A  Cable Cove Inn**, 201 Main St, **T** 7254236, www.cablecoveinn.com  A waterfront property right in town, with six beautiful and spacious rooms, some with their own hot tub, fireplace or deck. Beach access and continental breakfast included.

**B  Gull Cottage**, 254 Lynn Rd, Chesterman Beach, **T** 7253177, www.gullcottagetofino.com  A West Coast-style Victorian home in a forested area backing on to Chesterman Beach. Three fairly simple but nice en suite rooms. Guest lounge and hot tub. Full breakfast included.

**B  Water's Edge**, 331 Tonquin Park Rd, **T** 7251218, ironside@island.net  Another wonderful West Coast home with a fabulous common room offering the best views of all. Large en suite rooms, hot tub and staircase to tide pools. Breakfast included.

**B-C  Red Crow Guest House**, 1084 Pacific Rim Highway, **T** 7252275, www.tofinoredcrow.com  *Close to Botanical Gardens.* A splendid big house on the waterfront facing north, with views of the inlet islands, and set in old-growth forest. Three reasonable en suite rooms. Deck, forest trails, use of canoes and breakfast is included in the price.

## Hostel

**D-E  Whalers on the Point Guesthouse**, 81 West St, **T** 7253443, www.tofinohostel.com  Spanking new, HI-affiliated hostel with dorms and some private rooms. Very spacious with first-class facilities including kitchen, laundry, sauna and a wonderful solarium sitting room with harbour views. Discounts on tours and lessons. Reservation essential. Highly recommended.

## Camping

**F** **Greenpoint Campground** *19 km south.* The only campsite on Long Beach and easily the best one around. Small, but private and densely treed sites, some overlooking the beach. Operates on a first-come first-served system, and is heavily in demand, so arrive early. Dry toilets and no showers.

# Galiano Island

## Hotels

**AL** **Galiano Inn**, 134 Madrona Dr, **T** 5393388, www.galianoinn.com *Close to ferry.* One of the nicest lodges in Western Canada, built out of mighty wooden beams with lots of space. Decor throughout is sumptuous and romantic, with a beach and gardens to explore. Suites all have decks with ocean views, big beds, balcony, fireplace and luxurious baths. Breakfast in their plush restaurant, *Atrevida* (see p155), is included, as is a complimentary vehicle. Full spa costs extra.

**B** **Driftwood Village Resort**, 205 Bluff Rd E, **T** 5395457, www.driftwoodcottages.com *Set in a big garden near the ocean and ferry.* A large variety of pleasant, slightly rustic one- and two-bed cottages are available, all with decks and kitchens, some with fireplaces. Ferry pick-up. Great value.

**C** **Bodega Resort**, 120 Monastee Rd, **T** 5392677. *At west end of island.* Less easily reached, but set in beautiful, expansive grounds full of fruit trees and stone carvings on a ridge with far-reaching views. Spacious and comfortable log cottages sleep up to six. Horse riding available. Excellent value.

### B&Bs

**A** **Bellhouse Inn**, 29 Farmhouse Rd, **T** 1800-9707464, www.bellhouseinn.com   Set on the ocean close to the ferry, with expansive lawns, a sand beach and great views, this historic old farmhouse has three romantic rooms. Each has en suite bath and a balcony and great views.

### Camping

**F** **Montague Harbour Provincial Park**, **T** 3912300.   Halfway up the island is this wonderful oceanfront campground. The 15 walk-in sites have particularly good views. There are trails and beaches galore, but only dry toilets and no showers. Reservations are crucial in summer.

# Salt Spring Island

### Hotels

**B-C** **Harbour House Hotel**, 121 Upper Ganges Rd, **T** 5375571. A pretty standard hotel with ordinary, slightly faded rooms. Each has en suite bath and balcony. Good for price and location.

### Guesthouses and B&Bs

**A** **Quarrystone House**, 1340 Sunset Dr, **T** 5375980, www.quarrystone.com   *6 km from Vesuvius Bay*.   Sitting on a ridge by the ocean, with sweeping gardens and a large deck, the *Quarrystone* is great for views. The four lovely en suite rooms each have a balcony, fireplace, jacuzzi, TV/VCR and private entrance. Full breakfast included.

**B  Anchor Point**, 150 Beddis Rd, **T** 5380110, www.anchorpoint bb.com  *1 km south of Ganges*.  This pretty house set in forest and gardens has three well-appointed en suite rooms and a couple of smallish suites. There's a guest lounge, library, balcony and outdoor hot tub. Three-course breakfast and ferry pick-up included.

**C-D  Wisteria Guest House**, 268 Park Dr, **T** 5375899  *10 min walk from Ganges*.  The six rooms here, some with shared bath, cannot compare with some of the island's more sumptuous offerings, but the price is right and the location handy. There's a guest lounge, and breakfast, of course, is included.

## Hostel

**D-E  Salt Spring Island HI Hostel**, 640 Cusheon Lake Rd, **T** 5374149  *Open Mar-Oct*.  Situated on four forested hectares, within walking distance of beaches and Cusheon Lake, this very popular and friendly hostel has dorms and private rooms in a cedar lodge, plus three teepees and two small but delightful (and heavily booked) treehouses. Shared kitchen and common room. Very helpful staff. The only problem is getting there. Bike and scooter hire available.

## Camping

**F  Ruckle Provincial Park**, Beaver Point Rd, **T** 3912300  *9 km east of Fulford Harbour at the end of Beaver Point Road*.  The eight spots for RVs are nothing special, but those with a tent can walk in and claim one of the 70 sites dotted along the shore, with exquisite views of Swanson Channel. One of the most magical camping experiences in Western Canada, but no facilities.

With more restaurants per capita than any other Canadian city, it's worth treating your taste buds to something special in Vancouver. But that doesn't have to mean spending a lot of money. Reflecting Vancouver's cosmopolitan population, first-class examples of most international cuisines can be found – especially Italian, French, Greek and East Indian – and the city's large Oriental population fuels a staggering number of cheap Chinese, Vietnamese and sushi joints. A good way of getting the most out of Vancouver is to tour some of the many bars, bistros and restaurants, enjoying a drink and small dish in each. Kitsilano and Downtown are the best areas for top-of-the-range spots, the former also offering the broadest variety for vegetarians. West Broadway and Commercial Drive are also great for menu-browsing, but for sheer diversity it's hard to beat the West End streets of Robson, Denman and Davie. Most of the plush hotels have formidable restaurants, mentioned here only if exceptional in some way.

**$**

**Price**

### Eating codes

| | |
|---|---|
| $$$ | $40 and over |
| $$ | $26-40 |
| $ | $25 and under |

Prices refer to the average price of a main course.

A current trend in Vancouver is for 'fusion' food, with many top chefs blurring all international boundaries to create their own eclectic and imaginative dishes. Usually such blends entail a cuisine typical to Vancouver, best described as Pacific Rim or West Coast. Pacific Rim cuisine covers regions as far apart as BC, Japan, California and Australia. The emphasis is very much on healthy eating, using fresh, local, preferably organic ingredients prepared with understated simplicity. Another key factor is seafood. The fruits of the sea don't get much fresher than here, and some of Vancouver's finest restaurants specialize in presenting them in exciting new ways. West Coast cuisine has also added elements from traditional Native cooking. Salmon is used extensively, often prepared on cedar planks or alder grills. Fresh wild game such as caribou and buffalo is also featured, often flavoured with local berries. Barbecuing and smoking are very common. Weekend brunches are another Vancouver institution and well worthwhile. In Chinatown the choice is intimidating, but it's hard to go wrong. Food tends to be authentic Szechwan, and servings are large. For a snack try one of the numerous bakeries for a curried beef, BBQ pork or honey bun; they quickly become addictive.

# Downtown and Yaletown

## Restaurants

$$$ **Bacchus**, 845 Hornby, **T** 6085319. *In the Wedgewood Hotel. 0600-1430, 1800-2200. Map 2, E8, p250* The interior of this upmarket restaurant is plush, opulent and romantic: all dark wood, brass and burgundy, silver and crystal, with a piano, fireplace and cigar room. The food is classic French with a very good reputation. Sunday brunches, afternoon tea and cocktail hour are popular specialities. Reservation recommended.

$$$ **Blue Water Café and Raw Bar**, 1095 Hamilton, **T** 6888078. *Mon-Fri 1130-2300, Sat-Sun 1100-2300. Map 2, H8, p251* Upmarket but casual, spacious interior with brick walls, big wooden columns, leather chairs and sofas, soft lighting and jazzy music. Open kitchen serves mainly seafood and steak. Large selection of wines and beers.

$$$ **C Restaurant**, 1600 Howe, **T** 6811164. *On False Creek. 1130-1430, 1730-2300 (summer and Christmas); 1730-2300 (rest of the year). Map 2, I5, p251* Some of the best seafood you'll find anywhere. A broad range of choices, prepared in exciting new ways. Great wine list includes many sakes. Large, open and airy interior with views that are even better from the more intimate upstairs balcony. Recommended.

$$$ **Cioppino's Mediterranean Grill and Enoteca**, 1133 Hamilton, **T** 6887466. *1730-2300. Map 2, H8, p251* First-class Italian cuisine in two neighbouring rooms, one strictly formal, the other slightly more casual, both very stylish.

$$$ **Diva at the Met**, 645 Howe, **T** 6027788. *0630-1030, 1100-1530, 1730-2200. Map 2, G7, p251* A contender for the best in

★ **Breakfast**

Best

- Café Deux Soleils, p147
- Elbow Room, p133
- Homer St Café, p133
- Slickity Jim's Chat'n'Chew, p147
- Sophie's Cosmic Café, p142

town. Classic nouvelle cuisine with a West Coast attitude, prepared with flair and creativity. Decor is bright and elegant, sophisticated but not stuffy. Main courses feature one of every type of fish and meat. Taster menu is your choice of three downsized main courses for $60. Or try the cheese taster menu. Extensive wine list, many offered by the glass.

$$$ **Il Giardino Di Umberto**, 1382 Hornby, **T** 6692422. *Mon-Fri 1200-1500, Mon-Sat 1730-2300. Map 2, H5, p251* Top-notch Tuscan cuisine. Wonderful interior with sloping ceilings, terracotta walls, bright tasteful art, lots of plants and racks of wine. Several rooms of differing sizes and a tiled, enclosed garden patio that must be the nicest in town. Extensive wine list.

$$$ **Joe Forte's Oyster House**, 777 Thurlow, **T** 6691904. *Mon-Sat 1100-2230, Sun 1100-2200. Map 2, D7, p250* A beautifully opulent hall, dominated by a large horseshoe bar and furnished with brass banisters, wrought iron, marble columns, high ceilings and huge mirrors. The menu focuses on seafood, especially oysters. Great selection of beers and an award-winning wine list. Live piano music every night. Roof garden with smoking lounge and fireplace.

$$$ **La Terrazza**, 1088 Cambie, **T** 8994449. *1700-2300. Map 3, H1, p253* Italian cuisine done West Coast style, focusing on game and fish, using fresh ingredients like mixed organic greens and wild

mushrooms. Tiles and murals dominate the modern, Mediterranean setting.

$$$ **Le Crocodile**, 909 Burrard, **T** 6694298.  *Mon-Fri 1130-1400, Mon-Sat 1730-2300.*  *Map 2, E7, p250*  Sophisticated yet simple French-influenced cuisine. The ambience is upmarket bistro and the prices are reasonable for food of this calibre.

$$$ **Piccolo Mondo**, 850 Thurlow, **T** 6881633.  *Mon-Fri 1200-1400, Mon-Sat 1800-2200.*  *Map 2, E7, p250*  Italian food that forgoes the pizza and pasta in favour of fish and meat. Small, intelligent  menu, great wine list, and decor that is refreshingly simple and elegant.

$$ **Bin 941**, 943 Davie, **T** 6831246.  *Mon-Sat 1700-0200, Sun 1700-2400.*  *Map 2, G6, p251*  Small and intimate bistro with quirky decor, a lively atmosphere and inspirational tapas.

$$ **Desalvio's**, 1030 Davie, **T** 6843343. *1730-2200.*  *Map 2, F6, p250*  Casually elegant Spanish joint that has a loyal local following for its authentic food, big portions and reasonable prices.

$$ **La Bodega Tapas Bar**, 1277 Howe, **T** 6848814.  *Mon-Sat 1700-2400, Sun 1700-2300.*  *Map 2, G6, p251*  Long-standing favourite with a quiet, romantic atmosphere, good sangria, and food that is consistently rated as the town's best Spanish.

$$ **Rodney's Oyster House**, 1228 Hamilton, **T** 6090080.  *Mon-Wed 1130-2300, Thu-Sat 1130-2400, closed Sun.*  *Map 2, I8, p251*  Classic converted warehouse with brick walls and wooden beams. Downstairs is casual with stools at the bar, upstairs a little smarter. Well-heeled, slightly older clientele, but the ambience is lively and crowded. Focusing on oysters, mussels and chowder, the food is excellent, and the selection of wine and beers is good.

$$ **Simply Thai**, 1211 Hamilton, **T** 6420123. *Mon-Fri 1130-1500, Mon-Sat 1700-2300*. *Map 2, I8, p251* Owned by the Thai chef, whose food is highly recommended. Interior is bright with pale pastel walls, cream leather couches, graceful curved wood lines and simple brick and concrete floor. Considering such style and the well-heeled clientele it attracts, the prices are surprisingly reasonable.

$ **Urban Monks**, 328 Nelson, **T** 6691311. *1200-2100*. *Map 3, H1, p253* Vegan 'Zen' cuisine. Many options, all healthy. Suitably simple but tasteful decor.

## Cafés and fast food

$ **The Elbow Room**, 560 Davie, **T** 6853628. *0800-1600*. *Map 2, H7, p251* Popular breakfast place, famous for its large portions and the abuse regularly dished out to customers who fail to polish off their plates.

$ **Fritz**, 718 Davie, **T** 6840811. *Mon 1200-2000 , Tue-Wed 1200-2300, Thu 1200-0200, Fri-Sat 1200-0300, Sun 1200-2200*. *Map 2, H7, p251* Large portions of fries enlivened by a choice of a dozen different dips.

$ **Homer St Café**, 892 Homer, **T** 6872228. *Mon-Fri 0600-1700, Sat 0800-1200*. *Map 3, G1, p253* Basic cheap breakfast spot overflowing with genuine character.

$ **The Templeton**, 1087 Granville, **T** 6854612. *Sun-Thu 0900-2300, Fri-Sat 0900-0100*. *Map 2, G7, p251* Authentic old-fashioned diner. Colourful and fun, with very good comfort food.

$ **The Blunt Bros**, 317 W Hastings, **T** 6825868. *Sun-Wed 1100-2100, Thu-Sat 1100-2300*. *Map 3, E3, p252* Calling itself 'a respectable joint', this is the main bastion of attempts to sell

Vancouver as the new Amsterdam. Smoking is permitted and large amounts of paraphernalia sold, but there's no booze. Spacious interior with lots of sofas. Live music, mainly acoustic, Wed-Sat.

$ **Café Ami**, 885 W Georgia in the *HSBC* building, **T** 6880103. *Mon-Fri 0600-1730. Map 3, E1, p252* Easily the most pleasant spot for a coffee Downtown.

$ **Don't Show the Elephant**, 1207 Hamilton, *Mon-Wed 1400-2400, Thu-Sat 1400-0100, Sun 1300-2400. No phone. Map 2, H8 p251* Bright and trendy tea salon/gallery with a kind of oriental/futuristic feel that might be too self-consciously arty for some tastes, but gets top marks for originality.

# Gastown, East Side and Chinatown

## Restaurants

$$$ **Borgo Antico**, 321 Water, Gastown, **T** 6838376. *Mon-Fri 1200-1500, Mon-Sat 1730-2300. Map 3, D3, p252* Spacious and classy, with a number of very attractive rooms. Upstairs has big arched windows with views of the North Shore.

$$$ **Water Street Café**, 300 Water, Gastown, **T** 6892832. *1130-2300. Map 3, E3, p252* Elegant, classy room with massive windows and outdoor seating. Mainly pasta with some steak and seafood.

$$ **Buddhist Vegetarian Restaurant**, 137 E Pender, Chinatown, **T** 6838816. *1100-2030. Map 3, F5, p252* As well as regular vegetarian fare, they do a fine job of replicating meat-based dishes.

$$ **Incendio Pizzeria**, 103 Columbia, Gastown **T** 6888694. *Daily 1200-1500, Sun-Thu 700-2230, Fri-Sat 1700-2300. Map 3, E5, p252*

Also at 2118 Burrard. Rustic wooden tables in a large space that's colourful and casual. First-rate wood-oven pizzas.

$ **Hon's Wun-Tun House**, 268 Keefer, Chinatown, **T** 6880871. *1100-2300. Map 3, G6, p253* The obvious choice, having for some time scooped up most awards for best Chinese, best restaurant under $10, etc. Cafeteria-style decor, huge menu.

$ **Kam's**, 509 Main, Chinatown, **T** 6695488. *0930-2000. Map 3, E5, p252* Equally reliable, but smaller, with a more authentic feel.

## Cafés and fast food

$ **Blake's**, 221 Carrall, **T** 8993354. *Mon-Fri 0700-1900, Sat-Sun 0800-1900. Map 3, E5, p252* Exceptional downbeat and tasteful coffee house with good music, beer on tap and a small cheap menu.

$ **Cafe Dolcino**, 12 Powell St, **T** 8015118. *Mon-Sat 0730-2300. Map 3, E5, p252* Perfectly situated on Maple Leaf Square, with a couple of tables outside to take in the attractive setting.

# West End and Stanley Park

## Restaurants

$$$ **Brass Monkey**, 1072 Denman, **T** 6857626. *Daily 1700-0200, Sat-Sun 1000-1500 for brunch. Map 2, C3, p250* Extravagantly idiosyncratic and lavish decor, featuring a glittery bar, wrought-iron chairs and plush velvet drapes. The menu is surprisingly understated, only hinting at the complex and delicious dishes that have torn many a local away from their former favourites. The great Martinis, the wine list and the affable host all contribute to a memorable experience.

$$$ **Café de Paris**, 751 Denman, **T** 6871418. *Mon-Fri 1130-1400, Mon-Sat 1730-2200, Sun 1730-2100. Map 2, A5, p250* Perfectly captures the look of a French bistro, simple but classic and elegant. Food is meat (rabbit, calf's liver, beef tartare, etc) expertly prepared in classic French style. Nice bar.

$$$ **CinCin**, 1154 Robson, **T** 6887338. *Upstairs. Mon-Fri 1100-1430, daily 1500-2300. Map 2, D7, p250* Maybe the best Italian food in town. The Mediterranean decor is warm and romantic, sophisticated and comfortable, with balcony seating for those summer evenings. Many awards, mostly for its wine list.

$$$ **Delilah's**, 1789 Comox, **T** 6873424. *Sun-Thu 1730-2200, Fri-Sat 1730-2300. Map 2, C3, p252* The atmosphere here is louche: tongue-in-cheek decadent with lots of red, velvet, and gold gilt. Crowded and noisy, good for people-watching and famed for its Martinis. Food is variable but can be first class.

$$$ **The Fish House**, 8901 Stanley Park Dr, Stanley Park, **T** 6817275. *1130-2130. Map 2, A1, p250* Atmosphere of a slightly faded summer house with lots of windows, and shades of terracotta and dark green. Garden patios are a popular spot in summer. Menu is mainly well-prepared seafood with some steak and other meat dishes. Oyster bar. Two-for-one dinner specials 1700-1800.

$$$ **Le Gavroche**, 1616 Alberni, **T** 6853924. *1730-2330. Map 2, B5, p250* Classic French cuisine served in an old house whose many small rooms make for an intimate, romantic atmosphere.

$$$ **Liliget Feast House**, 1724 Davie, **T** 6817044. *Wed-Sun 1700-2200. Map 2, D3, p250* First Nations specialities served in a beautiful cellar space with cedar columns and tables, West Coast art and seating designed by Arthur Erickson. Authentic regional

dishes cooked on an alderwood grill. The platter for two with salmon, caribou and fiddleheads is the obvious choice.

**$$$  Raincity Grill**, 1193 Denman, **T** 6857337.  *Daily 1700-2130 (or later), Sat-Sun 1030-1430 for brunch.  Map 2, C3, p250*  The place to go for top-notch West Coast cuisine. Ingredients are fresh, locally produced, organic when possible and employed with subtlety and panache. The decor is equally modern, elegant and understated, while the wine list focuses on BC's finest.

**$$$  The Teahouse**, Stanley Park at Ferguson Point, **T** 6693281. *1130-1430, 1700-2200. Map 2, C3, p250*  More genuinely classy than the *Fish House*, this too feels like a summer house, but far more bright and breezy, with lots of plants and big windows offering fabulous views of English Bay. The menu is cosmopolitan: Pacific Rim lobster ravioli, Peking duck, salmon tournedos.

**$$  Da Pasta Bar**, 1232 Robson, **T** 6991288.  *Sun-Thu 1130-2100, Fri-Sat 1130-2200.  Map 2, D6, p250*  Dark and intimate interior with big paintings. Portions are large, and at lunch all pastas are $7, wine and beer $4.

**$$  Gyoza King**, 1508 Robson, **T** 6698278.  *Daily 1730-0100, Sat-Sun 1130-1500.  Map 2, B5, p250*  Dark, atmospheric and very popular spot for small Japanese dishes and sake.

**$$  Just One Thai Bistro**, 1103 Denman, **T** 6858989.  *1130-2230. Map 2, C3, p250*  One of the more consistently praised Thai options in town.

**$$  Romano's Macaroni Grill**, 1523 Davie, **T** 6894334. *Sun-Thu 1200-2200, Fri-Sat 1200-2300.  Map 2, D4, p250*  Just another pasta and seafood joint, but housed in the spectacular Gabriola Mansion, a grand old stone house, with high ceilings, ornate fireplace, stained glass and plush furnishings. Surroundings fit for royalty at a price anyone can afford.

**$$ Sami's**, 1795 Pendrell (also 3365 Cambie, **T** 8723366), **T** 9157264. *Tue-Thu and Sun 1700-2200, Fri-Sat 1700-2300, closed Mon. Map 2, C3, p250* Small up-tempo favourites serving innovative Indian fusion food such as saffron-scented seafood paella or fire-roasted coriander salmon.

**$$ Tanpopo**, 1122 Denman, **T** 6817777. *1130-2200. Map 2, C3, p250* About the best of the mid-range sushi houses, and certainly the choice for all-you-can-eat.

**$$ Tapastree**, 1829 Robson, **T** 6064680. *Sun-Thu 1700-2230, Fri-Sat 1700-2330. Map 2, A4, p250* Large, casual but elegant space filled with tasteful art and a patio in front. Varied menu of wonderful tapas, maybe the best in town, at around $10 each.

**$ Hon's Wun-Tun House**, 1339 Robson, **T** 6850871. *1100-2300. Map 2, C6, p250* Incredibly huge and bustling, very popular. Same menu as in Chinatown, same cheap prices. Huge servings of authentic Szechwan food prepared in an open kitchen.

**$ Café Luxy**, 1235 Davie, **T** 6695899. *Mon-Fri 1100-2230, Sat-Sun 1000-2230. Map 2, E5, p250* Broad range of homemade pasta dishes served with Caesar salad and garlic bread for about $11.

**$ Stepho's Greek Taverna**, 1124 Davie, **T** 6832555. *1130-2330. Map 2, F5, p250* Not much to look at, but some of the best Greek food in town, generous portions and prices. Be prepared to queue.

*Eating and drinking*

**Best** ★ **Vegetarians**

- Banana Leaf Malaysian Cuisine, p144
- Greens and Gourmet, p142
- Sweet Cherubim, p148
- The Naam, p141
- Vij's, p144

## Cafés and fast food

**\$\$ Capers**, 1675 Robson, **T** 6875288. *Mon-Sat 0800-2200, Sun 0800-2000. Map 2, B5, p250* Vegetarian food, deli and bakery using fresh organic food.

**\$ Benny's Bagels**, 1780 Davie, **T** 6857600. *0800-2000. Map 2, C3, p250* Good coffee and a patio with unbeatable views of English Bay.

**\$ Bojangles Café**, 1506 Denman, **T** 6873622. *Mon-Fri 0600-1200, Sat-Sun 0700-1200. Map 2, A4, p250* One of the best coffee houses in town, a neighbourhood institution.

**\$ Hamburger Mary's**, 1202 Davie, **T** 6871293. *Sun-Thu 0800-0200, Fri-Sat 0800-0300. Map 2, E5, p250* Diner-style joint serving big gourmet burgers until late.

# Granville Island and Vanier Park

## Restaurants
**\$\$ Cat's Meow**, 1540 Old Bridge St, **T** 6472287. *Mon-Sat 1100-0100, Sun 1100-2400. Map 2, K4, p251* Burgers, pizzas, nice appetizers, good selection of beer and other drinks. Funky interior with leather tablecloths and comfy leather armchairs.

**Eating and drinking**

**\$\$ The Sand Bar**, 1535 Johnson St, **T** 6699030. *1130-2400. Map 2, J5, p251* Beautiful renovated warehouse with high ceilings, industrial metal trimmings and vast windows looking out over False Creek. Heated roof patio. Tapas and seafood, wood-grilled burgers and pizza. Fine selection of ales and wines.

### Cafés and fast food

**\$ Granville Island Coffee House**, on the boardwalk behind *The Sand Bar*, **T** 6810177. *0700-1800. Map 2, J5, p251* Cosy little spot away from the hustle and bustle.

# Kitsilano and Point Grey

### Restaurants

**\$\$\$ Bishop's**, 2549 W 4th Av, **T** 7382025. *Sun-Thu 1730-2130, Fri-Sat 1730-2200. Map 5, C5, p255* One of Vancouver's undenied finest, with an unblemished reputation for the food and wine list, but above all the warmth and hospitality of the owner/host. All ingredients are 100% organic and mostly grown locally. Menu changes weekly. Smart but casual house-like setting.

$$$ **Lumière**, 2551 W Broadway, **T** 7398185. *1730-2200. Map 5, E4, p255* Often cited as Vancouver's finest restaurant. The interior is elegant, almost intimidatingly stylish and modern. There is no à la carte, just tasting menus from $80-120 without wine, worth every penny. Bistro bar next door has tapas-style dishes at $12 a shot.

$$$ **Maurya**, 1643 W Broadway, **T** 7420622. *Mon-Fri 1100-1430, daily 1700-2300. Map 5, E8, p255* Innovative West Coast versions of classic Indian dishes in spacious and exquisitely high class surroundings. The chef will create a menu for you for $22 per person.

$$$ **Pastis**, 2153 W 4th Av, **T** 7315020. *1730-2200. Map 5, C6, p255* French nouvelle cuisine with a small, ever-changing menu using the freshest fish and meats. Taster menu is $65. Another of Vancouver's key players, with decor too casual to match the prices.

$$ **The Eatery**, 3431 W Broadway, **T** 7385298. *Sun-Thu 1630-2330, Fri-Sat 1630-0030. Map 5, D2, p255* Trendy, very popular spot for Japanese-Western fusion food. Recommended.

$$ **The Naam**, 2724 W 4th Av, **T** 7387151. *Open 24 hours. Map 5, C4, p255* The city's oldest vegetarian restaurant, good from breakfast to dinner, with generous portions. Simple interior and heated atrium-style patio. Live music every night from 1900-2200, jazz/folk/world, etc. Licensed, with beers on tap and wine by the glass or bottle at very reasonable prices. Lots of desserts. See also p177.

$$ **Nyala**, 2930 W 4th Av, **T** 7317899. *Sun-Thu 1700-2230, Fri-Sat 1700-2330. Map 5, C3, p255* Tasty Ethiopian food, mostly curries and stews, much of it vegetarian. Served on very large platters with no forks. Vegetarian buffet until 2100 on Sunday, Monday and Wednesday for $11. Beer on tap. Very reasonable prices.

**Eating and drinking**

$$ **The Ordinary Café**, 1688 4th Av, **T** 7428386. *Mon-Fri 1130-1430, daily 1730-2330. Map 5, D8, p255* Dark and romantic bistro, classier, more ambitious and expensive than most and very popular despite a poor location.

$$ **Sausi's Lounge and Grill**, 3005 W Broadway, **T** 7343005. *Tue-Sat 1630-0130, Sun-Mon 1630-2400. Map 5, E3, p255* Lively, spacious yet romantic decor, full of colourful art and rugs. Food ranges from tagine and Thai curry to gnocchi. Martinis, cocktails, a fine selection of ales and even a segregated cigar lounge.

$$ **Tangerine**, 1685 Yew, **T** 7394677. *Mon-Fri 1700-2300, Fri-Sat 1700-2400, Sun 1700-2200. Map 5, C6, p255* Eclectic and upmarket tapas-style dishes at moderate prices. West Coast-Asian fusion cuisine with lots of fish and veggie options. Small and trendy locale close to Kits Beach, very popular with locals.

## Cafés and fast food

$$ **Capers**, 2285 W 4th Av, **T** 7396676. *Mon-Sat 0800-2200, Sun 0800-2000. Map 5, C6, p255* A variety of hot and cold vegetarian dishes, mostly organic, sold by weight deli-style. Fresh juices and baking. Large outdoor seating area.

$$ **Greens and Gourmet**, 2681 W Broadway, **T** 7377373. *1100-2200. Map 5, E4, p255* A vegetarian refuge with a calming plant-filled interior. Lots of great salads and assorted hot dishes all at $1.50 per 100g.

$$ **Sophie's Cosmic Café**, 2095 4th Av, **T** 7326810. *Sun-Thu 0800-2100, Fri-Sat 0800-2200. Map 5, D66, p255* A Kitsilano institution, now too popular for its own good, with long queues for weekend brunch. Eccentric, diner-style decor and large portions.

$ **Benny's**, 2505 W Broadway, **T** 7319730. *Sun-Thu 0800-0100, Fri-Sat 24 hours*. *Map 5, E5, p255* Arty, trendy and quirky, with great music. Good for coffee, bagels and melts.

$ **Calhoun's**, 3035 W Broadway, **T** 7377062. *Open 24 hours*. *Map 5, E3, p255* Huge and lively coffee shop with a slightly rustic feel. Great coffee, juices, breakfasts and baking.

$ **Epicurean Café**, 1898 W 1st Av, **T** 7315370. *Mon-Sat 0730-2000, Sun 0730-1900*. *Map 5, C7, p255* Small, quietly stylish neighbourhood secret with some outdoor seating. Some of the best java in town, plus breakfast, panini, deli, gelati, etc.

$ **Terra Breads**, 2380 W 4th Av, **T** 7361838. *0700-1800*. *Map 5, D5, p255* Baking to die for: breads, croissants, muffins, cakes and sandwiches to eat in or take away.

# South and East Vancouver

## Restaurants

$$$ **The Cannery**, 2205 Commissioner, **T** 2549606. *Near Commercial Dr. 1730-2230*. *Map 1, G5, p249* Replica of a West Coast cannery with rustic decor, two fireplaces, ocean views and a romantic atmosphere. Recommended for its creative seafood dishes, with the best selection of fish in the city and one of the finest wine lists.

$$$ **Seasons in the Park**, Queen Elizabeth Park, **T** 8748008. *Mon-Sat 1130-1430, Sun 1030-1430, daily 1730-2130*. *Map 6, F5, p256* One of the most romantic, high-class choices in town, with a sumptuous interior and exquisite views. Fresh seafood and steak, good appetizers and brunch.

$$$ **Shady Island Seafood Bar and Grill**, 3800 Bayview, Steveston, **T** 2756587. *Sun-Thu 1100-2100, Fri-Sat 1100-2230. Map 6, K2, p256* Most stylish of the numerous fish and chip places by the water serving all manner of seafood and steak. Spacious pub-like space, beer on tap, outside seating.

$$$ **Tojo's**, 777 W Broadway, **T** 8728050. *1700-2200. Map 6, A4, p256* Hands-down the best (and most expensive) sushi restaurant in Western Canada with the freshest fish, best sake and most beautiful presentation.

$$$ **Vij's**, 1480 11th Av, W Broadway, **T** 7366664. *1730-2200. Map 6, A1, p256* The only Indian restaurant that is regularly cited as one of the city's best overall eateries, with skilful, innovative variations on old favourites. No reservations.

$$ **Afghan Horsemen**, 445 W Broadway, **T** 8735923. *Sun-Thu 1730-2230, Fri-Sat 1700-2300. Map 6, A5, p256* Intimate, exotic decor, featuring lots of plants and ethnic art, and the chance to sit on the floor on rugs. Extremely popular and highly regarded.

$$ **The Amorous Oyster**, 3236 Oak, **T** 7325916. *Mon-Sat 1730-2200. Map 6, C3, p256* Cute Parisian-style bistro with very reasonably priced seafood dishes such as Cajun seafood wellington and baked oysters.

$$ **Banana Leaf Malaysian Cuisine**, 820 W Broadway, **T** 7316333. *1130-1500, 1700-2200. Map 6, A3, p256* Beautiful decor with traditional works of art hung on bright yellow walls, and lots of plants. Wonderfully tasty food, including many veggie and seafood options. Recommended.

$$ **Bukowski's Bistro**, 1447 Commercial Dr, **T** 2534770. *Mon-Sat 1700-0100, Sun 1700-2400. Map 1, G4, p256* An atmosphere worthy

of the name and large portions of food that never disappoint. Lively bar at the back, live jazz Monday, Thursday and Saturday, poetry readings and lectures on other nights. See also p177.

**\$\$** **Delgado's**, 3711 Bayview, Steveston, **T** 2755188. *1130-1430, 1700-2100. Map 6, K2, p256* The village's best restaurant, but with limited sea views. Beautiful, very Mediterranean interior, with lots of plants and a garden patio. Entrées include paella, cedar-plank salmon, grilled steak with roquefort, rustic lamb shank. Broad range of tapas at \$5-10.

**\$\$** **Havana**, 1212 Commercial Dr, **T** 2539119. *Mon-Thu 1100-2400, Fri-Sat 1100-0100, Sun 1000-2400. Map 1, G4, p249* Good for breakfast through to dinner and tapas, but most notable for its lively atmosphere and heated patio, one of the best places to watch the world go by. Interesting decor with graffiti scratched into the walls, and black and white photos of Cuba.

**\$\$** **Latin Quarter**, 1305 Commercial Dr, **T** 2511144. *Sun-Thu 1730-2400, Fri-Sat 1730-0130. Map 1, G4, p249* Tapas, paella and sangria in a crowded, party atmosphere with frequent live music.

**\$\$** **Locus Café**, 4121 Main St, **T** 7084121. *Mon-Sat 1000-0030, Sun 1000-2400. Map 6, E7, p256* Dark and brooding interior, with red and black walls and some wacky art. Almost too popular, especially

*Eating and drinking*

with the young, alternative crowd. Equally good for food or a drink, with a few good beers on tap. Menu is mainly predictable, with a few surprises like ostrich. Portions are large.

$$ **Monsoon**, 2526 Main St, **T** 8794001. *Daily 1700-2300, Sat-Sun 1030-1430, Fri-Sat 1700-0100.* Map 6, A7, p256 Full of colour and character, this trendy favourite specializes in gourmet multi-Asian fusion cuisine at reasonable prices. Appetizers like masala fries with banana ketchup for $4. Mains include a five-spice duck leg comfit with fancy trimmings for $15.

$$ **Pink Pearl**, 1132 E Hastings (Commercial Dr), **T** 2534316. *Daily 0900-1500, Sun-Thu 1700-2200, Fri-Sat 1700-2300.* Map 1, G4, p249 Dim sum here is an experience to savour: sit down and choose from the trolleys that drift by laden with goodies. Also noted for seafood.

$$ **The Whip**, 209 E 6th Av (Main St), **T** 8744687. *Daily 1600-0030, brunch 1000-1600 weekends.* Map 6, A7, p256 Funky little downbeat and arty café/pub with art scattered around. Salads, pan-seared yellow fin tuna with chipotle BBQ sauce sandwich, curries and pastas, and some great, cheapish beers on tap. Look for the old Tetley sign outside.

$ **Habibi's**, 1128 W Broadway, **T** 7327487. *Mon-Sat 1700-2300.* Map 6, A2, p256 Vegetarian Lebanese food, comprising lots of small tapas-style dishes. Smart, pleasant interior, nice atmosphere and beer on tap.

$ **On Lok**, 2010 E Hastings, **T** 2533656. *1100-0200.* Map 1, G4, p249 Enormous portions of reliably tasty Chinese food.

$ **Pajos**, 12771 7th Av, Steveston, **T** 2040767. *On the wharf. 1700-2100.* Map 1, K2, p249 Limited seating but arguably the best fish and chips in town.

$ **Punjabi Market** *Map 1, I4, p249*   Indiatown, also known as Punjabi Market, has a number of cheap restaurants specializing in all-you-can-eat buffets.

$ **Thai Away Home**, 1736 Commercial Dr, **T** 2538424. *1130-2100. Map 1, G4, p249*   Also at 1206 Davie (West End) and 3315 Cambie. Cheap but great Thai food in a very casual atmosphere.

## Cafés and fast food

$ **Café Deux Soleils**, 2096 Commercial Dr, **T** 2541195. *0800-2200/2300. Map 1, G4, p249*   Large vegetarian dishes, especially popular for breakfast. Friendly, rather alternative space with a play area for kids, and frequent live music.

$$ **Slickity Jim's Chat 'n' Chew**, 2513 Main St, **T** 8736760. *0800-1700. Map 6, B7, p256*   Small, popular place packed with weird and wonderful artefacts, an unbeatable choice for breakfast.

$ **La Casa Gelato**, 1033 Venables/Glen, **T** 2513211. *1000-2300. Map 1, G4, p249*   Tucked away in an unlikely spot is Vancouver's finest ice cream emporium, with 198 flavours to choose from, and servers who are pleased to let you try before you buy.

$ **Lugz Coffee House**, 2525 Main, **T** 8736766. *0800-2200. Map 6, B7, p256*   Comfy, downbeat atmosphere with couches and outdoor seating. Some food and smoothies.

$ **Soma Coffee House**, 2528 Main, **T** 8731750. *Mon-Fri 0700-2200, Sat 0800-2200, Sun 0900-2100. Map 1, G4, p249*   Minimalist, arty interior attracting a trendy, alternative clientele. Coffee and tea, lots of magazines to browse or buy and some nice snacks.

**$ Sweet Cherubim**, 1105 Commercial Dr, **T** 2530969. *1000-2000. Map 1, G4, p249* Health-food grocery store with a café attached that has wonderful baking and samosas, juices, smoothies and great value dishes that are vegetarian, organic and often vegan. Full dinner for $9.

**$ Sweet Revenge Patisserie**, 4160 Main, **T** 8797933. *1900-0100. Map 6, E7, p256* French-style salon with silk antique wallpaper, lace and china. Lots of fancy teas and decadent desserts, all made with natural ingredients.

# North Shore

### Restaurants

**$$$ The Beach House**, 150 25th St, **T** 9221414. *At Dundarave Pier, West Vancouver. Mon-Sat 1100-2300, Sun 1030-1000. Map 1, F2, p248* Mainly seafood in a spacious, summery building with huge windows looking out on to English Bay.

**$$$ Beach Side Café**, 1362 Marine Dr, West Vancouver, **T** 9251945. *Mon-Sat 1130-1430, Sun 1000-1430, daily 1730-2200. Map 1, F3, p248* Award-winning fine dining and one of the best decks in town with views across to Stanley Park and Kitsilano.

**$$$ The Observatory**, Main Building, Grouse Mountain, **T** 9840661. 1700-2200. *Map 1, D4, p248* Fine West Coast cuisine with the bonus of magnificent views. Reservations are essential, entailing a free gondola ride.

**$$$ Hiwus Feasthouse**, Blue Grouse Lake, Grouse Mountain, **T** 9840661. May-Oct, 1900-2030. *Map 1, D4, p248* What better way to enjoy a summer evening than walking through the sub-alpine scenery of Grouse Mountain to this traditional cedar longhouse situated on an attractive lake? Nightly shows cost $65 per person and include native story-telling and legends, dancing, singing and a full dinner of Pacific Northwest Native cuisine. Reservations essential by 1630 the previous day.

$$ **The Eiffel Café**, 4390 Gallant Av, Deep Cove, **T** 9292373. *Tue-Thu and Sun 1730-2030, Fri-Sat 1730-2130, Closed Mon. Map 1, F7, p248* French fusion creations in bright, elegant surroundings. Best of a few choices in the area.

$$ **Moustache Café**, 1265 Marine Dr, **T** 9878461. *Tue-Fri 1130-1430, Mon-Sat 1730-2200. Map 1, F3, p248* Also at 2526 Main, **T** 8794001. A casually stylish house-like setting, with eclectic, Mediterranean-influenced cuisine often cited as the North Shore's finest.

$$ **Raglan's Bistro**, 15 Lonsdale Av, **T** 9888203. *Handily located next to the quay and market. Wed-Sun 1730-2200. Map 1, F4, p248* Small and elegant with a nice menu of Mediterranean dishes.

### Cafés and fast food

$ **West of Java**, 105 1st St E/Lonsdale Av, **T** 9833467. *Mon-Fri 0630-2100, Sat-Sun 0700-2000. Map 1, F4, p248* Small and comfy coffee shop.

# Squamish and Garibaldi Provincial Park

### Restaurants

$$ **Red Heather Grill**, 37081 Cleveland Av, **T** 8922603. *At Howe Sound Inn. 1100-2200.* Great menu with creative West Coast food, nice salads and pizzas. The restaurant and pub have tasteful airy

decor and a lively ambience, with a patio offering priceless views of the Stawamus Chief. Their beers are also very good. Highly recommended.

## Cafés and fast food

$ **Sunflower Bakery Café**, 38086 Cleveland Av. *0800-1730*. Good coffee and freshly baked goods.

# Whistler

## Restaurants

$$$ **Araxi Ristorante and Pub**, **T** 9324540. *In the Square. 1730-2300*. With an excellent menu and high-class atmosphere, this is widely considered the best in town.

$$$ **Bearfoot Bistro**, 4121 Village Green, **T** 9323433. *1800-2100, 1800-2400 in high season*. Sumptuous surroundings. Taster menus are $85 for three courses. Wine bistro has à la carte menu featuring lots of game.

$$$ **Rim Rock Café**, Whistler Creekside, **T** 9325565. *South on Highway 99. 1800-2100*. A local favourite. Very comfortable and attractive interior, crab and lobster on the menu.

$$$ **Sushi Village**, **T** 9323330. *In The Westbrook. Fri-Sun 1030-1430, daily 1730-2200*. Top-notch sushi.

$$ **Caramba!**, 4314 Main St, Village North, **T** 9381879. *Sat-Sun 1130-1500, daily 1700-2200*. Incredibly popular, with a lively atmosphere and Mediterranean food such as calamari or wood-oven pizzas.

$$ **Kypriake Norte**, **T** 9320600, *opposite The Listel. 1600-2200.*
Possibly the best Greek/Mediterranean food in town, with great
specials and reasonable prices. Laid-back and friendly ambience.

$$ **La Bocca**, Village Square, **T** 9322112. *1000-2300.* Eclectic
West Coast fusion cuisine. Funky colourful interior with a nice bar.

$$ **La Brasserie des Artistes**, Village Square, **T** 9323569. *Next
door to La Bocca. 0800-2400.* A more laid-back atmosphere, lower
prices, and a great breakfast menu.

$$ **Uli's Flipside**, Creekside, **T** 9351107. *1700-2300.* Open and
colourful interior with good art. Menu covers anything from pasta to
paella to perogies, with good-value après-ski specials. Huge
portions. Good Martinis. Check out their brand new tapas bar *Casa*,
in St Andrew's House, Whistler Village.

## Cafés and fast food

$ **Gone Bakery and Soup Co**, **T** 9054663. *Behind Armchair
Books, next to the Liquor Store. 0700-2200.* Warm, cosy and
down-to-earth. A great spot for coffee, baking, soups, salads and
some meals.

$ **Ingrid's Village Café**, **T** 9327000. *Just off Village Square.
0730-1830.* Cheap breakfasts and lunches, homemade bread and
delicious sandwiches. Very popular.

# Victoria

## Restaurants

**$$$ Herald St Caffe**, 546 Herald St, **T** 3811441. *Wed-Sat 1130-1500, Sun 1100-1500, Sun-Fri 1730-2200, Fri-Sat 1730-2300.* Long-established favourite with locals. Creative gourmet food using fresh local ingredients in pleasantly busy, unpretentious surroundings. Great wine list.

**$$$ Restaurant Matisse**, 512 Yates St, **T** 4800883. *Wed-Sun 1730-2200.* High-class French cuisine in elegant, romantic surroundings.

**$$$ Wild Saffron**, 1605 Store St, **T** 3613150. *Wed-Sat 1700-2200.* Small but mouth-watering menu, combining West Coast and French cuisines. Simple but classy decor with lots of local art. Extensive wine list. Dinner only.

**$$ Ferris' Oyster Bar and Grill**, 536 Yates, **T** 3601824. *Mon-Sat 1130-2300, Sun 0900-2300.* Small, incredibly popular space with a great atmosphere, excellent food that concentrates on seafood, and reasonable prices. Highly recommended. Try their baked oyster platter.

**$$$ Il Terrazzo**, 555 Johnson St, **T** 3610028. *Mon-Fri 1130-1500, daily 1700-2200.* Authentic Italian food cooked in a wood oven. Huge menu and romantic atmosphere.

**$$ Lotus Pond Vegetarian**, 617 Johnson St, **T** 3809293. *Tue-Sat 1100-1500, 1700-2100, Sun 1100-1500, 1700-2000.* One of many Chinese restaurants, but 100% vegan.

$$ **Pagliacci's**, 1011 Broad St, **T** 3861662. *Sun-Thu 1130-1500, 1730-2200, Fri-Sat 1130-1500, 1730-2300.* Dark interior with a musical theme and frequent live music. Very intimate and usually packed. Italian food, wine, and great cheesecake.

$$ **Re-bar**, 50 Bastion Sq, T3602401. *Mon-Sat 0830-2100 (Fri-Sat in summer 0830-2200), Sun 0830-1530.* This funky, colourful, very popular old favourite serves a small menu of mostly vegetarian international dishes, such as curry, enchiladas, potstickers and lots of salads. There's also a fresh juice bar.

$$ **Siam Thai Restaurant**, 512 Fort St, **T** 3839911. *1130-1400, 1700-2100.* Stylish brick and wood interior, broad menu with surprisingly moderate prices.

$$ **Spinnakers Brewpub**, 308 Catherine St, **T** 3862739. *Across the Johnson St Bridge, or take the harbour ferry. 0700-2230 Sat-Sun.* Exceptional and very popular pub, where all food is prepared from scratch using fresh, local ingredients.

$$ **The Tapas Bar**, 620 Trounce Alley, **T** 3830013. *Mon-Thu 1130-2300, Fri-Sat 1130-2400, Sun 1100-2300.* A broad selection of mouth-watering tapas served in a colourful Mediterranean ambience featuring lots of art. Pleasant outdoor seating away from the traffic. Popular and recommended.

## Cafés and fast food

$$ **Willie's Bakery**, 537 Johnson St, **T** 3818414. *Mon-Wed 0700-1730, Thu 0700-2100, Fri 0700-2200, Sat 0730-2200, Sun 0730-1730.* Great baking and creative breakfasts for those who take the day's first meal seriously. Wonderful garden patio and organic coffee.

$ **Jaleen's**, 1320 Blanshard. **T** 3864442. *Mon-Fri 0700-1630, Sat-Sun 0900-1400*. Best coffee in town, good lunch menu.

$ **Torrefazione Italia Inc**, 1234 Government St, **T** 9207203, *Mon-Fri 0630-2100, Sat-Sun 0700-1900*. Great coffee and a nice place to hang out, with magazines and newspapers to browse.

# Tofino

## Restaurants

$$$ **Pointe Restaurant**, **T** 7253100. *0830-2100.   At the Wickaninnish Inn*. Excellent reputation for gourmet dining and spectacular panoramic ocean views. A nine-course meal with wine is $165. A drink in the lounge is more affordable and almost as gratifying.

$$$ **Raincoast Café**, 4th/Campbell St, **T** 7252215. *Wed-Sun 1730-2130*. Fast gaining a reputation as the place to eat. Cuisine is first-class Asian-West Coast fusion. Decor is stylishly minimalist, with an open kitchen.

$$$ **Schooner On Second**, 331 Campbell St, **T** 7253444. *0830-1500, 1730-2100*. Generally considered the best place for gourmet seafood, but also has some fine salads. Romantic atmosphere.

$$ **Alleyway Café/Costa Azul**, 305 Campbell St, **T** 7253105. *0700-2200*. Good breakfast option by day, great Mexican food in the evening. Airy, laid-back atmosphere and garden patio.

$$ **Café Pamplona**, **T** 7251237.  *At the Botanical Gardens, just south of town.   0800-1400, 1700-2200, closed Sun*.  Minuscule but mouthwatering menu that changes daily. Most ingredients come straight from their garden.

## Cafés and fast food

$ **Caffe Vicente**, 441 Campbell St, **T** 7252599. *Mon-Fri 0800-1600, Sat-Sun 0800-1500.* Upbeat café, with fancy sandwiches and cakes at moderate prices.

$ **The Common Loaf Bake Shop**, 180 1st St, **T** 7253915. *0800-2100.* A local institution and meeting place. Fresh baking, good coffee, and pizza. Bulletin board with useful information.

# Galiano Island

## Restaurants

$$$ **Atrevida**, 134 Madrona Dr, **T** 5393388. *At Galiano Inn. Sat-Sun 0730-1430, daily 1700-2100.* Delicious West Coast food in a gorgeous location with ocean views.

$$$ **La Bérengerie Restaurant**, Montague Rd, **T** 5395392. *Close to the park. Apr-Oct 1800-2100/2200, closed Wed.* Four-course set-menu French feasts. Advance reservation required. Also has an attractive and popular open-air café in July-August ($$).

# Salt Spring Island

## Restaurants

$$$ **House Piccolo Restaurant**, 108 Hereford Av, Ganges, **T** 5381844. *1700-2100.* Highly regarded gourmet cuisine in casual but smart surroundings.

**$$ Moby's Marine Pub**, 124 Upper Ganges Rd, **T** 5375559. *Mon-Thu 1000-2400, Fri-Sat 1100-0100, Sun 1100-2400.* A fine pub, popular with locals and one of the more reliable bets for food. Try the teriyaki salmon burger.

## Cafés and fast food

**$ Salt Spring Roasting Co**, Fulford Harbour, **T** 6532388. *Mon-Fri 0600-1800, Sat 0700-1800, Sun 0800-1800.* A nice local hang-out with a patio; and Ganges, 109 McPhillips Av, **T** 5370825. *Mon-Sat 0630-1800, Sun 1200-1700.* Good art on the walls and some decent baking and snacks.

**$ Tree House Café**, 106 Purvis Lane, Ganges, **T** 5375379. *0800-1500.* Tiny but hugely likeable establishment with baking, coffee and small meals, outdoor seating, live music most nights.

Most of the best venues are Downtown or within easy walking distance in Yaletown and Gastown, the latter definitely having the edge on nightlife. Vancouver really comes to life at the weekends, when many places will have live music and possibly a small cover charge.

The Vancouver bar and club scene is less lively than it could and should be, mainly due to a set of outdated licensing laws that led the *Georgia Strait* to describe this as the "city that fun forgot". A positive side-effect of laws requiring bars to serve food was the burgeoning of a thriving bistro/tapas culture and a whole panoply of funky venues serving drinks with tasty dishes thrown in. It's now  easier to get a drink without having to eat, and bars can stay open till 0400, though most still close around 0100. For the short-term visitor there are more than enough good drinking holes to experience, catering to all tastes.  Beer aficionados should definitely sample some of the excellent local microbrews, many produced right on the premises.

Almost all clubs operate from 2100 to a disappointing 0200 and charge a cover of $5-10, with drinks on the pricey side. Certain bars (such as *DV8*) stay open later than the clubs and can be more lively. Most venues listed here tend to host DJs spinning radically different music every night, which affects the atmosphere and clientele, making generalizations almost impossible. As elsewhere, house seems to be the main club staple, but you'll also find plenty of funk, soul, hip hop, reggae, jazz and top 40. For an overview of the scene, look out for the quarterly magazine *Nitelife*. For more specific night-to-night details consult the indispensable *Georgia Strait* or the useful www.clubvibes.com

# Downtown and Yaletown

### Bars

**DV8**, 515 Davie, **T** 6824388. *Mon-Thu 1700-0300 , Fri-Sat 1700-0400, Sun 1700-0200. Map 2, H7, p251* Dark, funky, rather louche bar, with interesting, progressive music and art displays. Belongs in a hipper, savvier city like San Francisco or Amsterdam. Popular with a trendy, alternative crowd, with DJs playing hip, modern sounds till late.

**The Lennox**, 800 Granville/Robson, **T** 4080881. *Sun Thu 1100-2400, Fri-Sat 1100-0100. Map 3, F1, p252* Standard pub with some outstanding but overpriced beers. Located on Downtown's busiest corner, the small patio is an ideal spot for watching the city rush by.

**Lucy Mae Brown**, 862 Richards, **T** 8999199. *Mon-Sat 1730-0100, Sun 1730-2200. Map 3, F1, p252* Stylish favourite with the young and trendy crowd. Downstairs a hip and modern Martini bar plays trip-hop-style music. Upstairs is an expensive restaurant with a Pacific Rim menu.

**Nelson Café**, 655 Nelson, **T** 6332666. *Mon-Wed 1500-0200, Thu and Sun 1100-0200, Fri-Sat 1100-0300. Map 2, G8, p251* Small, cosy and unpretentious, with a wooden floor and brick walls, decent inoffensive music and a mixed crowd. Good for a quiet pint and brunch and burgers.

**The Railway Club**, 579 Dunsmuir, **T** 6811625. *1200-0200. Map 3, E2, p252* Long-standing, down-to-earth upstairs bar, cosy and atmospheric with lots of wood, knick-knacks and intimate corners. Varied live music every night but Sun, cover about $6-8.

**Section (3)**, 1039 Mainland St, **T** 6842777. *Mon-Wed 1100-2400, Thu 1100-0100, Fri-Sat 1100-0200. Map 3, H1, p253* Decor is hip and arty, very modern and interesting: high, silver booths, hardwood floor, weird art and artefacts and wrought-iron stools at the curved bar. This and the funky music attract a more hip and savvy crowd than the usual Yaletown yuppies. Heated patio. Food covers all sorts from yam fries and baked brie to calamari and salads.

**Soho Café**, 1144 Homer, **T** 6881180. *Mon-Thu 1100-0100, Fri 1100-0200, Sat 1200-0200, Sun 1200-0100. Map 2, H8, p251* Stylish, unpretentious pub kitted out in brick and wood, with simple, rustic tables. Beer, billiards, food, tea and coffee.

**SuBeez Café**, 891 Homer, **T** 6876107. *Mon-Sat 1130-0100, 1130-2400 Sun). Map 3, G1, p253* Vast, open warehouse-style space with very high ceilings and huge concrete pillars. Dim lighting and weird art, including big screens showing silent B&W films. Music is equally odd, making for a strange and compelling atmosphere. Large selection of good draught beers and non-alcoholic drinks. Some overpriced food, including breakfast; better for drinks.

**The Sugar Refinery**, upstairs at 1113 Granville, **T** 6832004. *1700-0200. Map 2, G7, p251* Refreshingly quirky little place that feels like

★ **Hip spots**

**Best**

- Alibi Room, Gastown, p162
- Lucy Mae Brown, Downtown, p159
- Honey Lounge, Gastown, p 163
- DV8, Downtown, p159
- Section (3), Yaletown, p160

someone's living room. No two tables or chairs the same, all sorts of visual oddities scattered around, including the menu. Good beers on tap and extremely varied, generally off-the-wall live music almost every night. Attracts an alternative, predominantly young crowd.

## Clubs

**Crush**, 1180 Granville, **T** 6840355. *Mon-Thu 1900-0100, Fri-Sat 1700-0100. Map 2, G7, p251* Calling itself a 'Champagne Lounge', this plush spot aims for an older, wealthier clientele. Music is lounge, R&B, jazz and soul. Queues common.

**Drink Nite Club**, 398 Richards, **T** 6871307. *2100-0200. Map 3, E3, p252* Big dance floor, pumping music system and video screens, the varied music nights here are popular with a fairly young party crowd.

**Element Sound Lounge**, 801 Georgia St, **T** 6690806. *2100-0200. Map 3, E1, p252* Fancy club aimed at the upmarket Martini set. Top DJs play funk, techno, house, etc.

**Ginger 62**, 1219 Granville, **T** 6885494. *2100-0200. Map 2, H7, p251* Trendy spot for the young and beautiful people to show off their outfits and moves.

**Luv-A-Fair**, 1275 Seymour, **T** 6853288. *2100-0200. Map 2, H7, p251* Massive club with varied music, often alternative, retro, disco or theme-based.

**Plaza Club**, 881 Granville St, **T** 6460064. *2100-0200. Map 3, F1, p252* One of the classiest of the DJ-led party-atmosphere dance hot-spots, with one of the best sound and lighting systems in town. Very popular on Saturday nights.

**Voda**, 783 Homer, **T** 6843003. *2100-0300. Map 3, F1, p252* Stylish, elegant interior aimed at an older, more upmarket clientele. Music could be soul, funk, R&B or Latin.

**Wett Bar**, 1320 Richards, **T** 6627707. *2100-0200. Map 2, I7, p251* Huge, cavernous club with high ceilings, projection screens, dance floor and thumping music attracting young ravers or alternative.

# Gastown, East Side and Chinatown

### Bars

**Alibi Room**, 157 Alexander, **T** 6233383. *Sat-Sun 1000-1200, Sun-Wed 1700-2400, 1700-0100 Thu-Sat). Map 3, E5, p252* Owned and frequented by movie people, this is a seductively hip and happening hot spot. The atmosphere is exciting and trendy without being pretentious or intimidating, the music is modern, well chosen, and loud. Their small menu is also as exciting and innovative as any in town, at surprisingly reasonable prices.

**The Cambie**, 300 Cambie St, **T** 6846466. *1100-0100. Map 3, E3, p252* A favourite for those who like their boozers gritty, down-to-earth and friendly. Huge and smoky with a crowded summer patio. Big selection of cheap beer and food, and pool tables.

★ **Most up for it clubs**

**Best**

- Lotus Cabaret, Gastown, p163
- Plaza Club, Downtown, p162
- Wett Bar, Downtown, p162
- Drink Nite Club, Downtown, p161
- Sonar, Gastown, p164

**Honey Lounge**, 455 Abbott St, **T** 6857777.  *Sun-Thu 1100-2300, Fri-Sat 1100-2400.  Map 3, F4, p252*  Hip and dark bar, big and open, with impossibly comfortable couches smothered in huge velvet cushions and a good Martini list. Loud, upbeat, conversation-killing music makes for a club-like atmosphere without the dancing. *Milk Bar* next door is a trendy gay bar. See p163 and p215.

**The Irish Heather**, 217 Carrall St, **T** 6889779. *Sun-Thu 1130-2300, Fri-Sat 1130-0200.  Map 3, E5, p252*  An upmarket and authentic Irish bar and bistro, with a fine selection of ales. Tasteful, intimate interior with a glass conservatory at the back. Frequent live Celtic music and a menu featuring fancy reworkings of Irish staples.

## Clubs

**Lotus Cabaret**, 455 Abbott St, **T** 6857777.  *2200-0200.  Map 3, F4, p252*  Unpretentious, happening little club with low ceilings, attracting a young, friendly, energetic crowd that keeps dancing till close. House music most nights. Not exactly Gastown, but close enough. The *Honey Lounge* and *Milk Bar* are upstairs.

! The *X-Files* were filmed exclusively in Vancouver. You can take an *X-tour* (see p27) or visit the *Alibi Room* (see p162), co-owned by Gillian Anderson

**Bars and clubs**

**Purple Onion**, 15 Water St, **T** 6029442, www.purpleonion.com *2100-0200*. *Map 3, E5, p252* Two fairly intimate rooms; usually one has a DJ playing dance tunes and the other has a live band. Mixed, generally unpretentious crowd.

**Shine**, 364 Water St, **T** 4084321. *2100-0200*. *Map 3, E3, p252* Smart, colourful and intimate club with varied DJ-led music, attracting a fairly well-heeled 20-30 crowd. One to dress up for.

**Sonar**, 66 Water St, **T** 6836695. *2100-0200*. *Map 3, E4, p252* Attractive basement space with brick walls and wooden floors. One big area for bands/dancing and another for lounging. Music varies nightly from house to hip hop to reggae.

# West End and Stanley Park

### Clubs

**Balthazar**, 1215 Bidwell, West End, **T** 6898822. *1700-0200*. *Map 2, D3, p250* Spacious restaurant and lounge that stays open and busy till late with two separate rooms where DJs spin progressive house and more mainstream sounds.

# Granville Island and Vanier Park

### Bars

**Backstage Lounge**, 1585 Johnson, **T** 6871354. *In the Arts Club. Mon-Sat 1200-0200, Sun 1200-2400*. *Map 2, J4, p251* Airy and down-to-earth spot with a lively patio, decent food and live music almost every night from 2200 ($5 cover). Popular with students from Emily Carr.

★ **Down-to-earth**

**Best**

- Nelson Café, Downtown, p160
- The Railway Club, Downtown, p160
- The Cambie, Gastown, p162
- The Backstage Lounge, Granville Island, p164
- Soho Café, Yaletown, p160

**Dockside Brewing Co**, 1253 Johnston St, **T** 6857070. *In the Granville Island Hotel. 1700-2230/2400. Map 2, K5, p251* A hidden gem away from the hordes, with comfy leather armchairs and fine in-house beers. Wood-oven pizza and seafood.

# Kitsilano and Point Grey

## Bars

**Bin 942**, 1521 W Broadway, **T** 7349421. *1700-0200. Map 5, E8, p255* Thin room stuffed with weird and wonderful pieces of art. Trendy and lively, with modern but mellow dance music. Reasonable beer selection and an incredible menu of involved, delicious tapas.

**Elwood's**, 3143 W Broadway, **T** 7364301. *Mon-Thu 1600-0200, Fri 1300-0200, Sat-Sun 1100-0200. Map 5, E2, p255* Small wooden floored pub with downbeat feel. Good selection of beer and Martinis. Some nice starters and a few main courses at reasonable prices.

**King's Head**, 1618 Yew St, **T** 7386966. *0830-0100. Map 5, B6, p255* Cosy neighbourhood pub with a classic English feel. Lots of wood and an upstairs balcony area with intimate nooks and crannies. Frequent live acoustic-style music.

**Bars and clubs**

**Lou's Grill and Bistro**, 3357 W Broadway, **T** 7369872. *Mon-Sat 1100-0200, Sun 1100-2400. Map 5, E2, p255* Largish trendy bar/restaurant with terracotta walls, interesting art and a patio. Dim lighting, jazzy music and a great selection of beer on tap.

**Truffles Bistro**, 1943 Cornwall, **T** 7330162. *Sun-Thu 1700-0100, Fri-Sat 1700-0200. Map 5, B7, p255* Comfy couches, gentle music, tapas-style dishes and decadent hot chocolate.

---

### Clubs

**Mesaluna**, 1926 W Broadway, **T** 7335862. *2100-0100. Map 5, E7, p255* Latin club that's a lot of fun for dancing. Live salsa big band Fri and Sat nights.

# South and East Vancouver

**Public Lounge**, 3289 Main St, **T** 8731944. *Sun-Thu 1700-2400, Fri-Sat 1700-0100. Map 6, C7, p256* Casual, downbeat bar with a mainly young and bohemian clientele. Small but interesting cheap menu and some well-chosen (and cheap) microbrewed beers.

**WaaZuBee Café**, 1622 Commercial Dr, **T** 2535299. *Mon-Fri 1130-0100 Sat-Sun 1100-0100, Sun 1100-2400. Map 1, H5, p249* Large, comfortable space, dark, atmospheric and arty, playing loud upbeat music. Wide selection of beers and good food served in large portions. Best place for a drink on the Drive.

# North Shore

**Bars**

**The Raven**, 1052 Deep Cove Rd, **T** 9293834. *1100-2400*. *Map 1, F7, p248* Spacious, English-style neighbourhood pub with the best selection of draft beers in town. Lots of malt whiskies too. And the food comes in mammoth portions. Live music once or twice a week. Understandably popular.

**The Rusty Gull**, 175 E 1st St, **T** 9885585. *1100-2400*. *Map 1, F5, p248* Lively neighbourhood pub with good ales on tap, decent food, and frequent live music. Magical views from the patio of the city with shipyards and derelict warehouses in the foreground.

# Squamish and Garibaldi Provincial Park

**Bars**

**Howe Sound Inn**, 37081 Cleveland Av, **T** 8922603. *Sun-Thu 1100-2400, Fri Sat 1100-0100.* The only real choice. Top-notch pub with views of the Stawamus Chief, good food and great beers brewed on the premises.

# Whistler

**Bars**

There are plenty of very busy pubs around the village, most offering live music every weekend in the winter. For weekly listings pick up a free copy of *This Week*.

**Amsterdam Café**, Village Square, **T** 9328334. *1100-0100.* The most atmospheric bar in town. Small, quite dark, full of character and with a genuinely European feel.

**Boot Pub**, **T** 9323338. *In the Shoestring Lodge. 1500-0030/0200.* Down-to-earth boozer mostly frequented by locals. Various acts, from dancing girls to some decent bands.

**Brewhouse Restaurant and Pub**, **T** 9052739. *By Blackcomb Way in Village North. Sun-Wed 1130-2400, Thu-Sat 1130-0100.* Decent selection of microbrews and a great patio for people-watching.

**Mallard Bar**, **T** 9388000. *In the Château. Mon-Sat 1100-0100, Sun 1100-2400.* Very civilized and swanky spot for a quiet Martini.

## Clubs

**Maxx Fish**, **T** 9321904. *Below the Amsterdam. Mon-Sat 2100-0200, Sun 2100-0100.* Probably the best nightclub, with DJs playing mainly house, hip hop and funk.

**Tommy Africa's**, **T** 9326090. *Close to Village Square. Mon-Sat 2100-0200, Sun 2100-0100.* Attracts a younger crowd with hip hop style sounds.

# Victoria

## Bars

**Hugo's Brewhouse**, 625 Courtney St, **T** 9204844. *Mon-Sat 1130-0200, Sun 1130-2400.* Dark, somewhat industrial interior, very hip and popular. Clientele and mood changes through the day, turning into a thumping nightclub at 2200, playing mainly house music.

**Lucky Bar**, 517 Yates, **T** 3825825. *Mon-Sat 1700-0200, Sun 1700-2400*. Trendy, wacky little bar with live music or DJs nightly, usually very good and packed to the gills.

**Spinnakers Brewpub**, 308 Catherine St, **T** 3862739. *1100-2400*. Canada's oldest brew-pub. Great beer and food. Always packed. See also Eating p153.

**Suze**, 515 Yates, **T** 3832829. *Mon-Sat 1700-0200, Sun 1700-2400*. Very hip, dark and funky Martini bar with some outdoor seating. Small creative menu with international leanings.

**Swans Pub**, 506 Pandora Av, **T** 3613310. *Mon-Sat 1100-0200, Sun 1100-2400*. Best of the brew-pubs with a great selection of quality ales, a roomy yet cosy atmosphere and above all one of the best collections of West Coast aboriginal art you'll see anywhere. A magnificent establishment.

## Clubs

**Evolution**, 502 Discovery St, **T** 3883000. *2100-0200*. The only place for alternative sounds. Small, energetic, unpretentious venue for hard-edged and alternative music. Drink specials most nights.

**Hush**, 1325 Government St, **T** 3850566. 2100-0200. Small gay-friendly club attracting a young and likeable crowd. Gets some top DJs playing mostly house.

**Sugar**, 858 Yates, **T** 9209950. *Thu-Sat 2100-0200*. Probably the best club in town. Varied music, good lights and lasers; queues likely.

# Tofino and around

## Bars

**On the Rocks Lounge**, T 7253100. *At the Wickaninnish Inn, 1100-2300.* By far the nicest place for a sophisticated drink, with outstanding ocean views.

**The Marine Pub**, 634 Campbell St, T 7253277. *At the Weigh West Resort. 1100-2300.* The best choice in town, with good views and a few choices on tap.

# Galiano Island

## Bars

**Hummingbird Pub**, 47 Sturdies Bay Rd, T 5395472. *Sun-Thu 1100-2400, Fri-Sat 1100-0100.* Cosy pub with decent food (kitchen closes at 2100). The best place to meet locals.

# Salt Spring Island

## Bars

**Fulford Inn**, at Fulford Harbour, T 6534432. *1100-2330.* Nice pub with rooftop patio overlooking ocean. Basic pub food.

**Moby's Marine Pub**, 124 Upper Ganges Rd, T 5375559. *Mon-Thu 1000-2400, Fri-Sat 1100-0100, Sun 1100-2400.* A fine pub, popular with locals, good for food, and apparently the only place to experience locally brewed *Gulf Island Brewery* beers on tap.

All kinds of live music acts take to the city's many stages every night and there are some fine venues to choose from. The theatre scene is lively too, and for dance Vancouver is fast gaining a reputation as the country's second city after Montreal. British Columbians love going to the movies, and there are some excellent cinemas in town, whose repertoires go well beyond the usual Hollywood fare. A host of festivals through the summer keep the city's parks and beaches full of music, theatre and more. The first place to look for all weekly listings is the free *Georgia Strait* paper, available on major streets, in cafés and at venues. Tickets for most events are available through *Ticketmaster*, **T** 2804444. Half-price same-day tickets for many events are sold at the *Tickets Tonight* booth in the Visitor Information Centre, or online at www.ticketstonight.ca  *Arts Hotline* gives up-to-the-minute information at **T** 6842787, and www.AllianceForArts.com  is a weekly events calendar on the arts in Vancouver.

# Cinema

**Alcan Omnimax** in *Science World* at 1455 Quebec St, **T** 4437443. *Map 3, I5, p253* Wrap-around screen and sound, technologically the best venue in town.

**Blinding Light!!**, 36 Powell St, **T** 8783366. *Map 3, E5, p252* Microtheatre in the back of a café showing very serious, alternative films and documentaries.

**Denman Place Discount Cinema**, 1737 Comox, **T** 6832201. *Map 2, C3, p250* Cheap near-current shows and double-bills.

**Fifth Avenue Cinemas**, 2110 Burrard, **T** 2222991. *Map 5, D8, p255* Specializes in mainstream international films, with a good screen on which to see them.

**Granville Cineplex Odeon Cinemas**, 855 Granville St, **T** 6844000. *Map 2, F8, p250* The most convenient Downtown location but smallish screens.

**Hollywood**, 3123 W Broadway, **T** 7383211, www.hollywoodtheatre.ca *Map 5, E3, p255* Well-chosen and intelligently paired double bills for $5, usually quality films just off the first-run circuit, or less known but consistently worthwhile repertory choices. Shows usually change weekly.

**Imax**, Canada Place, **T** 6824629, www.imax.com/vancouver *Map 3, C2, p252* At least seven shows per day from noon. 40-minute documentary films $10.50, $8.50 concessions, feature films $12, $10 concessions.

**Pacific Cinematheque**, 1131 Howe St, **T** 6883456, www.cinematheque.bc.ca *Map 2, G7, p251* The main venue for rep, independent, art-house, foreign or just plain off-the-wall films. Shows change nightly. $9.25, $9.75/double bill, including membership fee. Also has a first-class film-reference library.

**Ridge Theatre**, 3131 Arbutus St/16th Av, **T** 7386311, www.RidgeTheatre.com  *Map 5, F6, p255*  The finest cinema in town. Built in 1950, this delightful venue is the last to still offer a glassed-in 'crying room' for parents with babies or noisy children. Double bills for $5 along the same lines as the *Hollywood*, but changing every two or three days.

**Tinseltown**, 88 W Pender, **T** 8060799.  *Map 3, F4, p252*  One of the best and most reasonably priced of the first-run cinemas.

**Van East**, 2290 Commercial Dr, **T** 2511313, www.vaneast.com  *Map 1, G4, p249*  Often shows the more intelligent of the first-run films.

# Comedy

**The Gastown Comedy Store**, 19 Water, **T** 6821727.  *Map 3, F4, p252*  Stand-up and improvisation.

**New Revue Stage**, 1601 Johnston St, Granville Island, **T** 7387013. *Wed-Thu 1930, Fri-Sat 2000, 2200 and 2345. $10-15.  Map 2, J4, p253*  Host of *Vancouver TheatreSports League*, six times world champions of comedy improvisation.

**Urban Well**, 888 Nelson, Downtown, **T** 6386070. 1700-0200 Sat-Thu, 1500-0200 Fri.  *Map 2, F7, p250*  Also 1516 Yew St, Kitsilano, **T** 7377770. Two large neighbourhood venues for stand-up comedy, as well as food, dancing or Martinis.

**Yuk Yuk's**, 750 Pacific Blvd, Downtown, **T** 6875233.  *Map 2, H6, p251*  The city's premier venue for stand-up comedy.

# Dance

**The Dance Centre**, **T** 6066405. With over 27 professional companies on its books, this is the best source of information.

**Scotiabank Dance Theatre**, 677 Davie, **T** 6890926. *Map 2, H7, p251* This, the only venue exclusively devoted to dance, mostly hosts contemporary works.

**Queen Elizabeth Theatre**, Hamilton/Georgia, **T** 2999000. *Map 3, E5, p252 See also p 176 and p178* The main venue for ballet.

**Vancouver East Cultural Centre**, 1895 Venables St, **T** 2549578. *Map 1, G4, p249 See also p177 and p180* Home of the innovative *Kokoro Dance Company*, **T** 6627441.

**Firehall Arts Centre**, 280 E Cordova, **T** 6890926. *Map 3, E6, p252 See also p179 and p185* Frequent dance venue, and home to the excellent annual *Dancing on the Edge Festival*, in July.

# Music

Most of the big names on tour stop in Vancouver, which also has countless smaller venues, with lots happening every night. Venues tend not to be faithful to one genre.

### Alternative and avant garde

**Brickyard**, 315 Carrall, Gastown, **T** 6853922. *Map 3, E5, p252* Smoky, rather sleazy venue for a variety of bands.

**The Cobalt**, 917 Main St, **T** 6852825. *Map 3, H6, p253* Punk, metal and hard core.

**The Sugar Refinery**, 1113 Granville upstairs, **T** 3311184. *Map 2, G7, p251* Alternative, avant garde, jazz or generally off-the-wall acts every night in a quirky setting.

**The Western Front**, 303 E 8th Av, **T** 8769343. *Map 6, A7, p256* Specializes in contemporary music, from jazz or electronic to world.

## Blues

**The Yale Hotel**, 1300 Granville, **T** 6819253. *Map 2, H6, p251* Divey bar that's the city's premier blues venue.

## Classical

**Chan Centre for the Performing Arts**, 6265 Crescent Rd, **T** 8222697. *Map 1, G1, p249* Mostly dedicated to classical performances, this UBC venue has three stages in one complex, the main hall being one of the city's finest.

**Orpheum Theatre**, 884 Granville St, **T** 6653050. *Map 2, F8, p250 See also p178* Home to the Vancouver Symphony Orchestra, the *Orpheum* hosts most major classical events. Built as part of the vaudeville circuit in 1927, it has an elegant Spanish Baroque-style interior with arches, tiered columns and marble mouldings.

**Queen Elizabeth Theatre**, Hamilton/Georgia, **T** 2999000. *Map 3, E5, p252 See also p175 and p178* Often plays host to opera and ballet.

## Folk and world

**Anza Club**, 3 W 8th Av, **T** 8762178. *Map 6, A6, p256* Antipodean hang-out, rather basic but with cheap beer and frequent live music.

**El Cocal**, 1037 Commercial Dr, **T** 4315451.  *Map 1, G4, p249*
Latin American restaurant with a laid-back, plant-laden
environment and frequent live music such as reggae, blues
and folk.

**Fairview Pub**, 898 W Broadway, **T** 8721262.  *Map 6, A3, p256*
Regular English-style boozer with folk music, often Celtic,
every night.

**Kino Café**, 3456 Cambie, **T** 8751988.  *Map 6, D5, p256*  Live
music every night, usually flamenco or salsa. No cover for diners.
Reasonable food, good beers.

**The Naam**, 2724 W 4th Av, **T** 7387151. *Map 5, C4, p255*
Restaurant with live music every night 1900-2200, usually acoustic
and worth checking out: jazz/folk/world, etc. See also p141.

**Vancouver East Cultural Centre**, 1895 Venables St, **T** 2549578.
*Map 1, G4, p249  See also p175 and p180*  A converted church and
intimate space popular for chamber music, dance, folk, etc.

**The Wise Hall**, 1882 Adanac, **T** 7363022, www.roguefolk.bc.ca
*Map 1, G4, p249*  Nice neighbourhood venue that's the main
focus for the *Rogue Folk Club*.

---

**Jazz**

**Bukowski's Bistro**, 1447 Commercial Dr, **T** 2534770.  *Map 1, G4,
p249*  Live jazz Mon, Thu and Sat.

**Hot Jazz Club**, 2120 Main St, **T** 8734131.  *Map 6, A7, p256*
Traditional jazz Tue, Sat and Sun, often big band. Oldest jazz
club in the city, as reflected in the run-down, Legion Hall decor.

**The Jazz Cellar**, 3611 W Broadway, **T** 7381959. *Map 5, E1, p255* Vancouver's principal jazz venue and a suitably atmospheric spot. Local or visiting musicians most nights. The food here is also very good.

**Jazz Hotline**, **T** 8725200, www.VancouverJazz.com

**Ouisi Bistro**, 3014 Granville St, **T** 7327550. *Map 6, C1, p256* Creole restaurant with a jazz attitude and live bands.

---

### Rock and pop

**Commodore Ballroom**, 868 Granville St, **T** 7394550. *Map 2, F8, p250* A wonderful old venue with a 1,000-seat capacity and a massive dance-floor built on rubber tyres.

**GM Place**, 800 Griffiths Way, **T** 8897889. *Map 3, H2, p253* Massive arena where the likes of Floyd or the Stones would probably play.

**Orpheum Theatre**, 884 Granville St, **T** 6653050. *Map 2, F8, p253 See also p176*

**Pacific Coliseum Concert Bowl**, PNE Grounds in Hastings Park, west of Highway 1, **T** 2804444. *Map 1, G5, p249* Where Britney Spears plays when she comes to town.

**Piccadilly Pub**, 620 W Pender, **T** 6823221. *Map 3, D2, p252* Thin, dark, smoky and packed. Live music most nights.

**Queen Elizabeth Theatre**, Hamilton/Georgia, **T** 2999000. *Map 3, E5, p252 See also p175 and p176* This 1960s modernist building with almost 3,000 seats hosts major rock and pop acts, as well as opera, ballet and musical.

**Richard's on Richards**, 1036 Richards, **T** 6876794. *Map 2, G8, p251* Attracts some of the best local and visiting acts and is a great venue to catch them: small and atmospheric with a brick wall as a backdrop behind the band, a balcony above for views, and arguably the best sound, lighting and sightlines in town.

**Vogue Theatre**, 918 Granville, **T** 2804444. *Map 2, F8, p250 See also p180* Receives big names, as well as a lot of tribute bands.

# Theatre

The two main focuses for theatre are Granville Island and the 'Entertainment District' of Downtown. The main season is October-April, but *Bard on the Beach* and *Theatre under the Stars* run continual shows through the summer (see Festivals, p186).

**Arts Club Granville Island Stage**, 1585 Johnston St, **T** 6871644. *Map 2, J4, p251* Small venue for casual theatre such as musical comedies.

**Centre in Vancouver for the Performing Arts**, 777 Homer St, **T** 6020616. *Opposite the Main Library. Map 3, F1, p252* Designed by the same architect, this state-of-the-art theatre is Vancouver's main Broadway-type venue for large-scale and popular theatre, dance and musicals.

**Firehall Arts Centre**, 280 E Cordova, **T** 6890926. *Map 3, E6, p252 See also p175* An operating firehall from 1906-75, the building now provides a small, intimate setting for quality dance and theatre.

**Pacific Theatre**, 1440 W 12th Av, **T** 2734659. *Map 6, B1, p256* Small but talented company presenting serious plays.

**Performance Works**, 1218 Cartwright St, Granville Island, **T** 6890926. *Map 2, K5, p251* Small-scale contemporary works of a generally high standard.

**Presentation House Theatre**, 333 Chesterfield Av, North Vancouver, **T** 9903474. *Map 1, F4, p248* Contemporary theatre and performance art in a 1902 school building.

**Stanley Theatre**, 2750 Granville/12th Av, **T** 6871644. *Map 6, B1, p256* An elegantly restored 1931 movie house, now an *Arts Club* venue for drama, comedy or musicals.

**Vancouver East Cultural Centre**, 1895 Venables, near Commercial Dr, **T** 2549578. *Map 1, G4, p249* Affectionately known as 'the Cultch', this converted Methodist Church is one of the best performance spaces in the city, thanks to great acoustics and sightlines and an intimate 350-seat capacity. It hosts a range of events, including theatre, music and dance, with an emphasis on the modern and sometimes controversial.

**Vancouver Playhouse**, Hamilton/Georgia, **T** 2999000 for information, **T** 6653050 for tickets. *Map 3, F2, p252* Fairly intimate venue for serious theatre, including many modern Canadian works.

**Vogue Theatre**, 918 Granville, **T** 2804444. *Map 2, F8, p250 See also p179* 1941 art deco-style building that has remained much the same, right down to the neon sign. Light-hearted pieces such as comedies and musicals

**Waterfront Theatre**, 1410 Cartwright St, Granville Island, **T** 6851731. *Map 2, K4, p251* Serious theatre in a renovated warehouse.

During the summer Vancouver celebrates with an almost continuous chain of events that make the most of the city's many fine beaches and parks. While the three-month Bard on the Beach and month-long Theatre under the Stars keep culture out in the open, just about every type of music has its time to shine. Perhaps the most important event is the 10-day Jazz Festival in June, one of the best of its kind in the country. July is the best overall time to come: topping a packed agenda are Celebration of Light, a two-week international firework competition, Dancing on the Edge, a highly regarded festival of original dance choreography, and the two-week Comedy Festival focused on Granville Island. The Fringe Festival in September is another major event, though not as celebrated as the one held in Victoria in August. If you're coming to ski, you could plan to catch the International Boat Show and Chinese New Year Festival in February, and Whistler hosts a steady stream of winter sports events. January is the best time to see bald eagles near Squamish, and late March sees the mass migration of whales past Tofino.

## January

**Polar Bear Swim**  Every New Year's Day since 1819 on English Bay Beach, lunatic locals have proven themselves by taking an icy dip. Watch if you can bear it.  **T** 6653424, www.city.vancouver.bc.ca

**Brackendale Winter Eagles Festival**  Incorporating the official Eagle Count, the festival will enjoy its 18th year in January 2004. Contact the Art Gallery for details. See p78.

**Big Mountain Experience** Features the Freeskiing Championships in Whistler in early-mid-January, www.freeskiers.org  Smaller events take place almost continually throughout the winter, including **Altitude**, **T** 1888-2584883, www.outontheslopes.com For information on all winter sports events, contact **T** 1800-7660449, www.whistler-blackcomb.com

## February

**Vancouver International Boat Show**  Held over four days in early February at BC Place, this is the largest and oldest boat show in Western Canada showcasing the latest vessels, gear and accessories.  **T** 2941313, www.sportsmensshows.com

**Chinese New Year Festival**  A 15-day party starting in early February, and including parades, live music, craft demonstrations and storytelling, mostly at the Dr Sun Yat-Sen Classical Chinese Garden. **T** 6623207, www.vancouver.about.com

**Peak to Valley Slalom Race**  Takes place  early in the month in Whistler. **T** 9052034.  Also in early February Whistler hosts a week-long **Gay Pride** event.

## March

**Canadian Alpine Championships** take place in Whistler in mid-March.

**Pacific Rim Whale Festival**  In Tofino during the last two weeks of March. Parades, boat races, storytelling, art shows and other events celebrate the annual migration of 24,000 grey whales past the West Coast. **T** 250-7267742, www.island.net/~tofino

## April

**International Wine Festival**  Over 40 events such as tastings and expensive dinners take place at various venues, but focused on the Vancouver Playhouse, involving 150 wineries from 15 countries.

**International Juvenile Ski Races** in Whistler, early April.

**Telus World Ski and Snowboard Festival**  In the third week of April in Whistler, this is the biggest annual winter sports event in North America. It is a huge 10-day party featuring free outdoor concerts, the world snowboarding championship and downhill skiing freestyle events. www.livelarge.ca

## May

**Cloverdale Rodeo**  Covering four days mid-month, this is the second biggest hoedown in the west after the Calgary Stampede, attracting cowboys from all over the continent to test their mettle in a number of traditional events. **T** 5769461, www.CloverdaleRodeo.com

**International Children's Festival**  Theatre, music, dance and puppetry from around the world turn Vanier Park into kid heaven for a week at the end of May, beginning of June. **T** 7085655, www.youngarts.ca

---

June

**Bard on the Beach Shakespeare Festival**  Shakespeare takes up residence in Vanier Park for three whole months starting in mid-June. Held in a ghetto of huge Elizabethan-style tents, these intimate performances are set with a stunning backdrop of mountains, ocean and city. **T** 7390559, www.bardonthebeach.org

**International Jazz Festival**  This 10-day event at the very end of June is one of the biggest of its kind in Canada, attracting many top names. Large and small acts occupy 40 stages around town, and there's a free two-day New Orleans-style street festival in Gastown. **T** 8725200, www.jazzvancouver.com

**Alcan Dragon Boat Festival**  Held around False Creek behind BC Place towards the end of June, this is a weekend of racing and Oriental cultural activities. **T** 6882382, www.canadadragonboat.com

**Squamish Adventure Festival**  A 10-day outdoor pursuits event including the 'Test of Metal' Mountain Bike Race.

**JazzFest International**  A 10-day event in Victoria at the end of June, with jazz, blues and world beat occupying 12 stages around town. **T** 3884233, www.vicjazz.bc.ca

---

July

**Dancing on the Edge**  A 10-day festival of contemporary dance. **T** 6890691, www.mcsquared.com/edge  See also p175.

**Vancouver Folk Music Festival**  Held at various venues over three days and nights in mid-July, this folk feast features local and international musicians and storytellers, with special events for kids. **T** 6029798, www.thefestival.bc.ca

**Theatre under the Stars**  Held in Stanley Park's open-air Malkin Bowl from mid-July to mid-August, this atmospheric event usually focuses on light musical shows. **T** 6870714, www.tuts.bc.ca

**Vancouver International Comedy Festival**  From late July to early August, Granville Island and selected other venues enjoy two weeks of diverse comedy acts from around the world. **T** 6830883, www.comedyfest.com

**Early Music Festival**  18 days from late July in the UBC Recital Hall. **T** 7321610, www.earlymusic.bc.ca

**Chamber Music Festival**  Also in late July, at Vanier Park's Crofton Schoolhouse, this series of concerts over 12 days features the finest young chamber musicians from Canada and abroad. **T** 6020363, www.vanrecital.com

**Caribbean Days Festival**  For two days at the end of the month, the North Shore's Waterfront Park is taken over with a colourful display of music, limbo, food, dance and arts. **T** 5152400, www.caribbeandaysfestival.com

**Celebration of Light**  A fortnight-long international fireworks competition starting in late-July. Each country puts on an hour-long show set to music. Fireworks are set off from a barge on English Bay. The most popular places for watching are the West End beaches, but Vanier Park is better. **T** 7384304.

**FolkFest**  At the very start of July in Victoria Inner Harbour and Market Square with nine days of performing arts, food, arts and crafts, fireworks, and a three-night-long world beat rave. **T** 3884728, www.icavictoria.or/folkfest.

**RootsFest**  Also in Victoria, this is a weekend-long festival in mid-July. Dozens of musicians, including some top names, offer a mixed bag of folk, reggae, blues, world, zydeco and other rootsy music. Camping available on site. **T** 3863655, www.rootsfest.com

**Victoria Shakespeare Festival**  From mid-July to mid-August, *Theatre Inconnu* give renditions of the Bard's work, designed to be accessible and affordable for all. Performances in an intimate 200-seat venue at the Heritage Theatre, St Ann's Academy, 835 Humboldt Street. Tickets are $14, $12 seniors, $10 children. **T** 3600234. www.islandnet.com/~tinconnu

## August

**Gay Pride Parade**  Held in the first week of the month, this is Vancouver's main gay and lesbian event, a colourful parade around the West End, followed by a massive party for all who want to join in the spirit.  **T** 6870955, www.gayvancouver.com  At the same time is **Out on Screen Queer Film Festival**, www.outonscreen.com, showcasing gay-themed or gay-directed movies from around the world (see also Gay and lesbian, p213).

**Powell Street Festival**  This 2-day event held in early August at Oppenheimer Park in 'Japantown' is a celebration of Asian Canadian culture and history, featuring dance, music, theatre, and lots of great food. **T** 7399388, www.shinova.com/powellfestival

**Abbotsford International Air Show**  Held in Abbotsford Airport over the second weekend of the month, this is the second largest air show in North America. State-of-the-art aircraft from around the world compete and perform. **T** 8528511, www.abbotsfordairshow.com

**Richmond Tall Ships Festival**  After the success of the wonderful 2002 festival, there are plans to hold it every three years, the next one being 2005. **T** 1877-2470777, www.richmondtallships.ca

**PNE Fair**  Starting in late August and running for about 18 days at the PNE Grounds in Hastings Park, the PNE Fair features live music and entertainment, exhibits, livestock and the Playland Amusement Park with some 40 fairground rides. **T** 2532311.

**Squamish Days Logger Sports**  Canada's biggest chainsaw bonanza in mid-August, with competitions, races, beef barbecue, gospel singing, a parade and hoedown: a real slice of life. **T** 8929244.

**Victoria Fringe Theatre Festival**  Straddling late August and early September, this is one of the best and oldest fringes in Canada, and the event for which Victoria is most famous. For 11 days, countless venues stage all manner of shows from noon to midnight. $5 for membership, $8 for indoor shows. **T** 3832664, www.victoriafringe.com

September

**Molson Indy**  Held around the east end of False Creek, with seating mostly in Concord Pacific Place, this major event includes a series of races, culminating in the final of the Indy-champ Car World Series Race. Tickets from $80-220 for all three days. **T** 2804639, www.molsonindy.com

**Vancouver Fringe Festival**  For 10 days in early to mid-September, some 100 international companies deliver 500 shows in indoor and outdoor venues, with Granville Island the obvious focus. **T** 2570350, www.vancouverfringe.com

**Vancouver International Film Festival**  Amidst much logistical mayhem, some 300 well-chosen films from 50 countries are shown to enthusiastic audiences at 17 theatres over the course of 17 days.  **T** 6850260, www.viff.org

## October

**International Writers (and Readers) Festival**  For five days in mid- to late October, 40 events featuring over 60 well- and lesser-known Canadian and international authors occupy four venues around Granville Island. **T** 6816330, www.writersfest.bc.ca

## November

**Vancouver Storytelling Festival**  Starting in early November is a month of events, concerts and workshops from top raconteurs. **T** 8762272, www.internetstore.bc.ca

**Aboriginal Film and Video Festival**  Held in the first week of the month, from Thursday-Sunday, at Van East cinema and other venues. The event showcases works by Native Canadians and other indigenous peoples from around the world. **T** 8710173.

**East Side Culture Crawl**  For three days at the end of the month, over 200 artists of all kinds open their studios to the public. Maps and information will be available at Strathcona Community Centre, 601 Keefer St. **T** 2154492,  www.culturecrawl.bc.ca

**Moving Pictures Film Festival**   Whistler, early to mid-November, shortly before the ski season begins, and gets everyone in the mood with a showing of mountain films as well as other Canadian independent productions. **T** 9383200.

---

December

**Festival of Lights**   Occupies almost the entire month at the VanDusen Gardens, 20,000 lights and displays add extra seasonal magic to this perennially beautiful place. **T** 8789274, www.vandusengarden.org

**Snow Scene**   Features the FIS Snowboard World Cup in Whistler, mid-December. **T** 7877770, www.snowscene.ca

Shopping

The best items to buy in Vancouver are locally made arts and crafts, which are often exceptional and very reasonably priced. Granville Island is the obvious place to start looking. Particularly popular are works by West Coast First Nations, such as carvings, jewellery, masks, paintings and prints, clothing and moccasins. There's a lot of mass-produced rubbish sold to tourists, so head to Gastown and shop around. Typically Canadian souvenirs include bottles of authentic maple syrup or smoked salmon (which will keep), often sold in attractive hand-crafted cedar boxes. Music lovers should note that this is one of the cheapest places in the world for CDs. It's also good for high-quality sporting equipment that's probably cheaper than at home. Antique hunters will find many stores on Main Street from16th to 20th Avenue and 26th to 28th Avenue, on Richards between Hastings and Pender, and further afield in the suburb of New Westminster. Vancouver's undisputed retail Mecca is Robson Street, though many more unusual speciality stores are found on Kitsilano's Fourth Avenue.

## Art and crafts

**Circle Craft**, The Net Loft, Granville Island, **T** 6698021. *1000-1800. Map 2, J4, p251* One of many fine stores gathered in The Net Loft opposite the Public Market, with a well-chosen selection of crafts in a variety of media and sizes.

**Crafthouse Gallery**, 1386 Cartwright St, Granville Island, **T** 6877270. *1030-1730. Map 2, K5, p251* Another great collection of quality works including pottery, textiles and jewellery.

**First Nations Creations Art Co-op**, 20 Water St, Gastown, **T** 6029464. *1000-1800 Map 3, E4, p252* Owned and operated by aboriginal artists, presenting contemporary, experimental works as well as more traditional stuff. Prices can be more reasonable than elsewhere.

**Gallery of BC Ceramics**, 1359 Cartwright St, Granville Island, **T** 6695645. *1030-1730. Map 2, K5, p251* Run by members of the Potters Guild of BC, this is *the* place for ceramics, with a large selection that changes monthly. Pieces range from the functional to the fantastical, and prices are generally reasonable.

**Hill's Native Art**, 165 Water St, **T** 6854249. *0900-2100. Map 3, E4, p252* 1008 Government St in Victoria, **T** 250-3853911. *0900-1730.* Three floors of the real thing, including masks, carvings and jewellery.

**Inuit Gallery**, 345 Water St, **T** 6887323. *Mon-Sat 1000-1800, Sun 1100-1700. Map 3, D3, p252* North America's most extensive purveyor of Inuit arts and crafts, including some very beautiful modern and traditional sculptures and prints.

**Industrial Artifacts**, 49 Powell St, Gastown, **T** 8747797. *Tue-Sat 1000-1800. Map 3, E5, p252* A stunning collection of furniture and art that has been ingeniously fashioned from reclaimed pieces of old industrial machinery and wood. Almost everything is painfully desirable.

**Rendez-Vous Art Gallery**, 671 Howe St, **T** 6877466. *Mon-Sat 1000-1730, Sun 1100-1700. Map 3, E1, p252* Stylish space with a wide range of work from many key contemporary artists. Anything from landscapes to a big collection of Inuit carvings.

**Spirit Wrestler Gallery**, 8 Water St, **T** 6698813. *Mon-Sat 1000-1800, Sun 1200-1700. Map 3, E5, p252* Works by major aboriginal artists, including some outstanding sculpture.

---

### Books

**Banyen Books and Sound**, 3608 W 4th, **T** 7327912. *Mon-Fri 1000-2100, Sat 1000-2000, Sun 1100-1900. Map 5, C1, p255* A huge, well-chosen selection that focuses on new non-fiction, particularly alternative lifestyles and spirituality. Also CDs.

**Chapters**, 788 Robson, **T** 6824066. *0900-2200. Map 2, F8, p250* Vast and handily located, this is the obvious place to head for new books of all kinds.

**Duthie Books**, 2239 W 4th Av, **T** 7325344. *Mon-Fri 0900-2100, Sat 0900-1800, Sun 1000-1800. Map 5, C6, p255* Though still broad, the repertoire here is more selective than at the ubiquitous *Chapters*, and the environment more conducive to browsing.

**The Great Canadian News Co**, 1092 Robson, **T** 6880609. *Mon-Thu 0700-2200, Fri-Sat 0700-2300, Sun 0700-2100.*

*Map 2, D7, p250*  Probably the biggest selection of magazines and foreign newspapers in town.

**Macleod's Books**, 455 W Pender, **T** 6817654. *Mon-Sat 1000-1730, Sun 1200-1700.*  *Map 3, E2, p252*  An intimidatingly large selection of used books, from the popular to the obscure.

**Munro's**, 1108 Government St, Victoria, **T** 250-3822464. *Sun-Thu 0900-1800, Fri-Sat 0900-2100.*  Widely celebrated as the most beautiful bookstore in Western Canada. The 24-ft coffered ceiling, stained-glass windows, wall-hangings and well-chosen art create an environment perfect for browsing.

## Clothes and accessories

Most of the international chains such as *Benetton*, *French Connection* and *The Gap* are found on **Robson Street**, mainly between Burrard and Jervis. **Granville Street** is better for off-the-wall new and used clothing and footwear, while the exclusive designer labels like *Chanel* and *Versace* are found on **West Hastings**. For less expensive but more original clothes **4th Avenue** in Kitsilano is a good bet.

**Aldo**, 128-1025 Robson, **T** 6832443. *Sun-Wed 1000-1900, Thu-Sat 1000-2100.*  *Map 2, E8, p250*  810 Granville, **T** 6058939. *Sun-Wed 1100-1900,Thu-Sat 1100-2100.*  *Map 2, F8, p250*  Fashionable but reliable shoes. The Robson branch has their newest most exclusive designs, the Granville store stocks yesterday's leftovers at discount prices.

**Deluxe Junk Co**, 310 W Cordova St, **T** 6854871. *Mon-Sat 1000-1800 , Sun 1200-1700. Map 3, E3, p252*  One of a handful of stores in Gastown selling funky used and retro clothing. An excellent (if pricey) selection.

**John Fluevog**, 837 Granville, **T** 6882828. *Mon-Wed 1100-1900, Thu-Fri 1100-2000, Sun 1200-1700.* *Map 2, F8, p250* Funky, artistic, but not necessarily practical shoes for both sexes.

**Lululemon**, 2113 4th Av, **T** 7326111. *Sat-Wed 1000-1800, Thu-Fri 1000-1900.* *Map 5, C6, p255* Unique locally made items that are designed for yoga, but have become incredibly popular here as fashion wear.

**Object Design Gallery**, 2072 4th Av, **T** 6830047. *1000-1800.* *Map 5, D6, p255* A distinctive jewellers, selling mostly silver items, all handcrafted by local artists and very reasonably priced.

**Pharsyde**, 2100 4th Av, **T** 7396630. *Tue-Sat 1000-1900, Mon 1100-1900, Sun 1100-1800.* *Map 5, D6, p255* Casual but wonderfully hip clothing and shoes for men and women.

**Roots**, 1153 Robson, **T** 6848801. *Mon-Wed 1000-1900, Thu-Fri 1000-2100, Sun 1100-1900.* *Map 2, D7, p255* Stylish casual wear, including clothes suitable for Canadian winters. Official makers of the clothes worn by Canada's Salt Lake City Olympic athletes.

### Department stores and shopping centres

**The Bay**, Granville/Georgia, **T** 6816211. *Mon-Wed 0930-1900, Thu-Fri 0930-2100, Sun 1100-1800.* *Map 3, E1, p252* Today's relic of the mighty Hudson's Bay Company sells just about everything for the house and wardrobe. Quality is high, prices reasonable, and they're forever having sales where genuine bargains can be found.

**Pacific Centre Mall**, Georgia/Howe, **T** 6887236. *Mon-Wed 0930-1900, Thu-Fri 0930-2100, Sat 0930-1800, Sun 1200-1800.* *Map 3, E1, p252* If you need to find something fast Downtown, this is the place, with many fashion and shoe stores like *The Gap*,

**Getting clammy in Chinatown**
*Shops sell all kinds of weird and wonderful ingredients, including geoduck (pronounced gooeyduck), the world's largest clam.*

*Banana Republic* and *Holt Renfrew*, old favourites like *The Body Shop*, useful stuff like *Lens and Shutter*, plus fast food and coffee.

## Gifts and souvenirs

For touristy souvenirs head to Water Street in Gastown. For more original ideas check out the speciality shops on 4th Avenue.

**Salmagundi West**, 321 W Cordova, **T** 6814648. *1030-1730. Map 3, E3, p252* A really fun shop, packed with eccentric off-the-wall oddities, toys and tit-bits.

**Vancouver Art Gallery Shop**, 750 Hornby St, **T** 6624706. *Map 2, E8, p250 Fri-Wed 1000-1800, Thu 1000- 2100.* Lots of inspiringly beautiful items.

## Markets

**Chinatown Night Market**, 200 Keefer St and E Pender, *1830-2300, Fri-Sun, Jun-Sep. Map 3, G6, p253* An open-air market that is even more bustling and fascinating than Chinatown's usual mayhem.

**Flea Market**, 703 Terminal Av/Main St, **T** 6850666. *Sat-Sun 0900-1700. Map 3, I6, p252* The best venue for bargain hunting, though most of what's sold is rubbish and you have to haggle hard.

**Granville Island Public Market**, **T** 6666477. *0900-1800. Map 2, J4, p251* A mouth-watering high-quality market stuffed with fresh produce, speciality foods and a BC wine store.

**Kids' Market**, 1496 Cartwright St, Granville Island, **T** 6898447. *0900-1800. Map 2, K4, p251* 25 stores just for children, much of the stuff is educational and handmade locally.

**Lonsdale Quay Market**, **T** 9856261. *Sun-Thu 0900-1830, Fri 0900-2100. Map 1, F4, p248* Handily located where the SeaBus arrives at the North Shore; a good second choice to Granville Island.

## Music

**A&B Sound**, 556 Seymour St, **T** 6875837. *Mon-Wed 0900-1800, Thu-Fri 2100, Sun 1100-1700. Map 1, F4, p248* The best place to go for new CDs. A large selection and you can listen before you buy.

**Black Swan**, 3209 W Broadway, **T** 7342828. *1100-1900. Map 5, E2, p255* New and used CDs and records of all kinds, including some rare items. Intelligent selection and knowledgeable staff.

**Charlie's**, 819 Granville, **T** 6882500. *Mon-Fri 1000-2200, Sat-Sun 1000-2000. Map 2, F8, p250* The biggest selection of cheap used CDs in town and a very central location.

**Zulu Records**, 1972 W 4th Av, **T** 7383232. *Mon-Wed 1030-1900, Tue and Fri 1030-2100, Sat 0930-1830, Sun 1200-1800. Map 5, D7, p255* The hippest CD store in town, with a broad selection of new and used music of all kinds. The emphasis is on modern or alternative sounds. Good for concert information and tickets.

---

## Sports and outdoor equipment

**Cheapskates**, 3644 W 16th, **T** 2221125; 3228 Dunbar, **T** 7341191; 3496 Dunbar, **T** 7341160. *Map 5, F1, p255 Mon-Thu 1100-1800, Fri 1100-1900, Sat 1000-1800, Sun 1100-1700.* Three stores in one area with a massive selection of used equipment.

**Mountain Equipment Co-op**, 130 W Broadway, **T** 8727858. *Mon-Wed 1000-1900, Thu-Fri 1000-2100, Sat 0900-1800, Sun 1100-1700. Map 5, C8, p255* The broadest and best selection in town, and often the best deals, though you have to pay a $5 membership fee first.

**Pacific Boarder**, 1793 W 4th Av, **T** 7347245. *Mon-Wed 1000-1800, Thu-Fri 1000-2000, Sat 1000-1800, Sun 1100-1700. Map 5, C8, p255* The most extensive of many ski and snowboard stores in this area.

**Sport Mart**, 735 Thurlow, **T** 6832433. *Mon-Sat 0930-2100, Sun 1100-1800. Map 2, D7, p250* Reliable all-round supplier conveniently located Downtown.

Shopping

All kinds of outdoor pursuits are available right on Vancouver's doorstep. Where else can you ski in the morning then swim, kayak or play a round of golf in the afternoon without even leaving town? While the skiing, mountain biking and diving are world class, for many people the most rewarding and accessible activities are hiking and kayaking. A number of great trails lead up to panoramic viewpoints in the foothills of the Coast Mountains, with even better hiking through spectacular landscapes further north on the Sea to Sky Highway. No previous experience is necessary to enjoy a first-rate kayaking adventure right from town. There is also ample scope for golfing, fishing and sailing. Squamish to the north is a centre for climbing and windsurfing. Whistler is a skier's haven, with many other winter and summer sports available. The Gulf Islands are perfect to tour in a kayak or yacht, while Tofino has some of the best kayaking and surfing in the country.

# Vancouver

## Hiking

Hiking in the Coast Mountains on the North Shore is prime, a real boon for Vancouver's inhabitants. Those described on  are the pick of the bunch.

## Kayaking

The best local kayaking is up Indian Arm, reached from **Deep Cove**. This 18-km fjord reaches deep into the Coast Mountains, passing old-growth forest and waterfalls, with ample chance to view wildlife. All the same, it still doesn't compare with some of the paddling available from Tofino. The second best local starting point is **Bowen Island**, from where the eight Paisley Islands can be visited as a day trip. **English Bay** and **False Creek** offer mellow paddling in the heart of the city. For rapids, head for the Capilano and Seymour Rivers.

**Bowen Island Sea Kayaking**, T 9479266, www.bowenisland kayaking.com  Rentals and guided trips. Full-day lesson $99. Three-hour tour $49. Rentals $50 per day.  Seven-hour tours of the Paisley Islands or Keats and Gambier Islands, $99. Sunset and full moon paddles. Lessons for all levels.

**Deep Cove Canoe and Kayak**, T 9292268, www.deepcove kayak.com  Tours of Indian Arm. $60 for three hour Natural History tour. $295 for two days, $50 for 2½-hour full-moon tour. Lessons $65 for three hours. Rentals.

**Ecomarine Ocean Kayak Centre**, Granville Island, **T** 6897575, www.ecomarine.com   Rent kayaks and a wide range of equipment. Lessons in the Aquatic Centre.

**Takaya Tours**, 3093 Ghum-Lye Dr, North Vancouver, **T** 9047410, www.takayatours.com   Tours of Indian Arm from Deep Cove with First Nations guides. Five hours per $75, full moon tours, three hours per $40.

## Mountain biking

There is a lot of first-class, hard-core mountain biking around Vancouver, not for the inexperienced. The three main areas, each with multiple tough trails, are Cypress, Seymour and Fromme Mountains. Trail maps of these areas ($6 each), along with some much-needed advice, are available at bike shops. See also *Mountain Biking BC* by Steve Dunn. Seymour is probably the least difficult of these, but Burnaby Mountain and Fisherman Trail are more appropriate rides for intermediates/beginners. Note that the law requires you to wear a helmet.

**Bayshore**, 745 Denman, **T** 6882453. Rents bikes and also rollerblades and strollers/pushchairs.

**Bike Cellar**,1856 W 4th, **T** 7387167. One of the many bike stores on West 4th Av and Broadway.

**Bush Pilot Biking**, **T** 9857886, www.bushpilotbiking.com   Contact Johnny Smoke for more detailed professional information or tours.

**Deep Cove Bikes**, 4310 Gallant Av, Deep Cove, **T** 9291918. *May-Sep only*. $30 per day for basic mountain bike, $50 (and a big deposit) for a serious bike.

**Simon's Bike Shop**, 608 Robson, **T** 6021181. The best store Downtown. Rentals are $19 per day, $69 per week. $55 per day for a hard-core mountain bike.

**Spokes Bicycle Rentals**,1798 W Georgia St, **T** 6885141. The pick of the bunch near Stanley Park. Road bikes, tandems, child trailers, baby joggers, etc. Regular bike $3.75 per hour, $15 per day; mountain bike $42 per six hours. Also guided bike tours.

## Skiing: cross-country

**Hollyburn Ridge** in Cypress Provincial Park, **T** 9220825, www.cypressmountain.com   Has 19 km of track-set trails including 7 km lit up at night, $15.

**Grouse Mountain** has 5.3 km of trails, lit at night.

**Sigge's Sport Villa**, 2077 W 4th Av, **T** 7318818. Has the biggest selection of cross-country equipment, plus lessons and rentals. They run shuttles to Lost Lake in Whistler on Saturday and Manning Park on Sunday.

## Skiing: downhill

**Cypress Mountain**, **T** 9265612, www.cypressmountain.com Geared towards more advanced skiers, with the largest vertical drop, and terrain that divides up as 23% beginner, 37% intermediate, 40% expert. Five chair lifts lead to 34 runs on two mountains, with night skiing on all runs. There is also a snowboard park with half-pipe, and 10 km of snow-shoeing trails. A SnowPlay area has tubing and tobogganing. All rentals are available, and lessons are given for skiing and boarding. There is a café and a lounge. A ski pass is $42. The hill is open daily 0900-2230.

**Grouse Mountain**, **T** 9809311, www.grousemountain.com  Has easy access, tremendous views, night-skiing, and the best facilities. A high-speed gondola takes you to the base, then other lifts fan out from there. There's also ice skating, snow-shoeing, and cross-country skiing. Day pass is $35/$19 senior/$25 youth/$15 child. Night-skiing from 1600-2200 is $26/$17 senior/$20 youth/$12 child. For a five-day pass, $139/$79 senior/$109 youth/$49 child.

**Kenny's Fun Club**, 1833 Anderson St near Granville Island, **T** 7384888. Rents snowboards for $29 per day.

**Mount Seymour**, **T** 9862261, www.MountSeymour.com  Good for beginners and snowboarders, with three snowboard parks. The Snow Tube Park is a glorified toboggan hill with a tow back up. $11 for two hours, including the tube. Snow-shoeing $17-20 including rentals. *Open 0930-2200 weekdays, 0830-2200 weekends.* Day pass $29/$24 senior/$14 child, with reduced rates from 1300 and 1600. Book of five tickets $119/$59 concessions. Ski rental $26/$15 concessions, snowboard rental $37/$31 concessions, package of lesson, lift ticket and rental is $61/$45 concessions. Shuttle bus from Lonsdale Quay $7/$5 return, $4/$3 one way. **T** 7187771 for schedule.

## Scuba diving

There is plenty of quality scuba diving close to Vancouver. Whytecliffe Park at the western tip of the North Shore, Cates Park in Deep Cove, and Porteau Cove on Highway 99 are all renowned underwater reserves, and the waters around Vancouver Island have been named the second best place to dive in the world by the Jacques Cousteau Society.

**BC Dive Adventures**, 228 W Esplanade, North Vancouver, **T** 9832232, www.bcdive.com  Recommended for courses, trips and rentals.

**Diving Locker**, 2745 W 4th Av, **T** 7362681, www.kochers diving.com  PADI diving instructors for 30 years. Beginner's course is $270 all-inclusive. A wide range of advanced courses available, as well as two- and three-day dive trips from $400; *Sunday Safari* day-trips for $100 including all the gear, and equipment rental ($50 per day for the works).

**Rowand's Reef Dive Team**, 1512 Duranleau St, Granville Island, **T** 6693483, www.rowandsreef.com  Also recommended for courses, trips and rentals.

**Water Sport Exchange**, 3291 W Broadway, **T** 7343667.  For used equipment.

---

### Swimming

The two best swimming spots in town are the large open-air pool at **Kits Beach** (see p54) and the professional-sized heated saltwater pool in the **Vancouver Aquatic Centre** at 1050 Beach Av, **T** 6653424. The latter also contains a fitness centre.

# Squamish and Garibaldi Provincial Park

---

### Hiking

First-class hiking is found throughout the Coast Mountain Range. For suggestions of the very best trails, see p80.

## Climbing

**Stawamus Chief**  Almost 300 routes traverse the 625-m face of the  Chief,  including the University Wall, considered the country's most difficult climb. But the Chief is only one of many venues around Squamish for **climbing**. **Smoke Bluffs**, for instance, also has over 300 routes of all levels. The most up-to-date book is *Squamish New Climbs* by Kevin McLane.

**Vertical Reality Sports Store**, 37827 2nd Av. A good source of information and also rents equipment. For instruction, contact Chris Lawrence, **T** 8928248.

**www.squamishrock.com**  A very handy on-line climbing guide.

## Mountain biking

There are countless mountain bike trails around Squamish, suitable for all levels up to the most extreme. Most are concentrated in the Smoke Bluffs and Crumpit Woods area east of town, or around Alice lake and the Garibaldi Highlands further north. The free *99 North* magazine contains some useful maps.

**Tantalus Bike Shop**, 40446 Government Rd/Highway 99, **T** 8982588. Bike rentals and key information.

## Windsurfing and kayaking

**Squamish Windsurfing Society**, **T** 9269463. Responsible for maintaining Squamish Spit, the most popular spot for windsurfing and whitewater kayaking, about 3 km north of Squamish along Government Road.  They charge a small fee. On a good day, this makes for a great spectator sport.

**Sea to Sky Ocean Sports**, 37819 2nd Av, **T** 8923366. For **kayak** rentals, $30 per four hours.

# Whistler

## Skiing

Between them, the two mountains of Whistler and Blackcomb offer skiers nearly 3,000 ha of terrain, featuring 12 bowls, three glaciers and 200 marked trails. Facilities on the two hills include at least 12 restaurants. Equipment can be rented from stores, hotels or on the mountain. The *Whistler Express*, *Fitzsimmons Express* and *Blackcomb Excalibur* gondolas all leave from the south side of the Village. The *Wizard Express* and *Magic Chair* lifts both head up to Blackcomb form the Upper Village.

**Affinity Sports** have a number of branches including the Village Square, the *Pinnacle Hotel*, the *Clocktower* and the *Blackcomb Lodge*. It is worth spending a little extra on high-performance gear.

**Mountain Hosts**, **T** 9323434. Free tours for intermediates to become familiar with the terrain. Daily at 1130 from the Guest Satisfaction Centre at the Alpine Lightboard on Whistler Mountain and from the Mountain Tour Centre at the top of the Solarcoaster Gondola on Blackcomb.

**Whistler Blackcomb**, **T** 9323434, www.whistler-blackcomb.com *0830-1500 mid-late Nov to Jun. $65/$32 concessions/free for 6 years.*

**Whistler Ski School**, **T** 1800-7660449. For beginners these mountains can be intimidating, so a lesson is recommended. The ski school is excellent and charges about $93 per day, $499 with a private instructor.

## Other winter sports

**Cross-country skiing** is best at Lost Lake, with 32 km of trails which are lit up at night, $10, **T** 9050071, www.crosscountryconnection.bc.ca The *Valley Trail* runs all over, linking the Village, Lost Lake, Alta Lake, Alpha Lake and beyond. There are also some good trails at the *Château Whistler* and *Nicklaus North* Golf Courses.

**Cougar Mountain**, 36-4314 Main St, **T** 9324086, www.cougar mountain.ca Can organize a variety of winter sports around Whistler including **back-country skiing**, much of it in Garibaldi Provincial Park. **Heli-skiing** starts at about $629 per day. Two-hour **dog-sledding** tours of the Soo Valley cost $125 per person per 2½ hours and leave four times daily. **Horse-drawn sleigh rides** leave hourly from 1700-2000 and cost $45 per person. **Snowmobile** tours for all levels start at $89 per two hours for a double. **Snow-shoeing** is possible just about anywhere. Tours start at $49 per two hours. **Winter fishing** starts at $139 per person per half day. **Helicopter sight-seeing** tours start at $149 per person for 20 minutes.

**Whistler Alpine Guides Bureau**, **T** 9383228, www.whistlerguides.com Arrange tours and instruction for skiing, snowboarding, ice climbing and mountaineering.

**Whistler Cross-Country Ski Centre**, **T** 9327711, www.whistlernordiccentre.com Cross-country skiing, and guided hikes ($99 per person per day) in summer.

**Whistler Valley Adventure Centre**, **T** 9386392, www.whistler adventure.com Also provide any of the above activities. Provides the same range og activities as *Cougar Mountain* (see above).

## Summer sports

Not long after Whistler Mountain closes in June, the Seventh Heaven Chair starts running up to the 45-ha Horstman Glacier on Blackcomb for summer skiing. Largely used by professionals and free-style clinics, there is also space for casual skiers ($39 day-pass). Once the snow has gone there is also some great **hiking** in Whistler (for recommended trails, see p80). Mountain bikers can carry their steeds on the lift up to **Whistler Mountain Bike Zone**, *open May-Sep*, which consists of 100 km of single-track trails. Lost Lake has 30 km of hiking/biking trails. There is **climbing** in Nordic Estates between the Village and Creekside. **Fishing** for trout and **swimming** are popular here and at a number of other nearby lakes. Alta Lake is good for **windsurfing**. Local tour operators will take you hiking, horse riding, jet-boating, fishing, bear-viewing, even on a **4x4 hummer** tour. Finally, Whistler has a growing reputation as a **golf** mecca, with many new and challenging courses designed by the likes of Jack Nicklaus and Arnold Palmer.

**The Great Wall Climbing Centre**, **T** 9057625, has two walls, one indoors at the *Westbrook Hotel*, another outside at the base of Blackcomb Mountain. They also arrange four-hour tours in July and August, $79 per person.

**Mountain Riders**, 4309 Skiers Approach, **T** 9323659. For mountain bike rentals.

**Whistler Bike Company**, 4050 Whistler Way, **T** 9389511. Within walking distance of the Village.

**Whistler River Adventures**, at the gondola, **T** 9323532. Organize river-rafting, $60 for two hours.

Sports

# Tofino and around

### Kayaking

There are plenty of guides in Tofino keen to take you out.

**Rainforest Kayak**, www.rainforestkayak.com  Offer eco-friendly lessons and tours.

**Remote Passages**, **T** 7253330, www.remotepassages.com  Offer day and evening paddles and will instruct beginners. One possibility is $58 for four hours, including a walk on Meares Island.

**Tofino Sea Kayaking Co**, **T** 7254222, www.tofino-kayaking.com Also do tours, and will rent to experienced kayakers.

# Salt Spring Island

### Kayaking and other activities

**Island Escapades**, 163 Fulford-Ganges Rd, **T** 5372537, www.islandescapades.com  A highly respected company for sailing, kayaking, hiking and climbing; rentals, lessons and tours.

**Saltspring Kayaking**, 2923 Fulford-Ganges Rd, **T** 6534222. Rentals of kayaks and bikes, tours and lessons.

**Sea Otter Kayaking**, 149 Lower Ganges Rd, **T** 5375678, www.seaotterkayaking.com  Rentals and three tours a day.

In keeping with their relaxed West Coast attitude, people in Vancouver are extremely tolerant of homosexuality and the city has become, like San Francisco, one of North America's gay capitals. A large number of bars, clubs and events are aimed specifically at a gay crowd and many more are proud to be seen as gay-friendly. The main focus of this lively and open gay scene is the West End (especially Davie Street), which houses the largest gay community in Western Canada. By dint of sheer proximity, Stanley Park, particularly Lees Trail near Second Beach, has become a popular cruising area. This whole zone is the venue for the main gay event of the year: held every August, the Gay Pride Parade is a colourful, extravagant celebration; a wild, joyful party to which all are welcome. At the same time is the Out on Screen Queer Film Festival, with gay-themed or gay-directed movies from around the world. There are always special events taking place around town, easily tracked down in *XtraWest*, Vancouver's free gay newspaper.

## Bars and clubs

**Club 23 West**, 23 W Cordova, **T** 6885351. *2100-0200. Map 3, E4 p252* Straight club with gay nights. Naked Heaven, once monthly, is for gay nudists. Every fourth Saturday is lesbian night.

**The Dufferin**, 900 Seymour, **T** 6834251. *Mon-Sat 1200-0200, Sun 1200-2400. Map 3, F1, p252* Rather seedy but safe, friendly, down-to-earth gay pub with 3 zones. The main bar has entertainment nightly, such as drag shows and strippers. Downstairs is a smoking area with go-go boys. And there's a silly but popular karaoke lounge.

**The Fountainhead**, 1025 Davie St, **T** 6872222. *Sun-Thu 1100-2400, Fri-Sat 1100-0100. Map 2, F6, p250* Pleasant gay-friendly neighbourhood pub, more upmarket than most. Popular heated and covered patio. Pub food.

**The Global Beat**, 1249 Howe St, **T** 6892444. *1800-0200. Map 2, G6, p251* Lounge and restaurant with lots of big, comfy chairs and couches, and relaxed but modern music.

**Milk Bar**, 455 Abbott, **T** 6857777. *1100-2300/2400. Map 3, F4, p252* Stylish gay bar, very artistically decorated with plush milk-coloured walls and furnishings. The gay-friendly *Lotus* club downstairs has a fetish night, the last Sat of every month. The *Honey Lounge* next door is popular with the lesbian scene at the weekends.

**Numbers Cabaret**, 1042 Davie, **T** 6854077. *2100-0200. Map 2, F6, p250* Heaving nightclub with queues to get in at the weekend. The main floor is for dancing and cruising, popular with a slightly older denim and leather crowd. Downstairs has some great speciality beers. Upstairs is more mellow, with pool tables.

**The Oasis Pub**, 1240 Thurlow St, **T** 6861724.  *Sun-Thu 2100-2400, Fri-Sat 2100-0100.  Map 2, F6 , p250*  Gay-friendly upmarket piano bar.

**The Odyssey**, 1251 Howe St, **T** 6895256. *2100-0200.  Map 2, G6, p251*  The city's main gay club with high-energy dance music, good DJs and sometimes strippers. Attracts the youngish gym crowd. Large outside covered and heated terrace.

**The Pump Jack**, 1167 Davie, **T** 6853417.  *1800-2400.  Map 2, F5, p250*  A friendly bar frequented by the leather community, gay and straight.

## Beaches

**Wreck Beach**, *Map 1, H1, p249*  Vancouver's nude beach, has a gay section. Go to the main beach at UBC (Gate 4) and head south.

**Sunset**, *Map 2, F3-H4, p250-51* and **Second**  *Map 4, F2, p254* beaches are also gay friendly.

## Bookshops

**Little Sister's Book and Art Emporium**, 1238 Davie, **T** 6691753. *1000-2300.  Map 2, E5, p250*  Gay and lesbian bookstore. A great place for information.

**Womyn's Ware**,  896 Commercial Dr, **T** 2542543. *Mon-Wed and Sat 1100-1800, Thu-Fri 1100-1900, Sun 1100-1700.  Map 1, G4, p249*  Informative, friendly, community-oriented store selling books, sex-toys and more.

## Cafés

**Sugar Daddy's**, Davie St. T6321646. *Mon-Thu 0700-2400, Fri-Sun 0700-0200. Map 2, E5, p250* Gay-friendly neighbourhood coffee bar.

## Festivals

**Gay Pride Parade**, T 6870955, www.gayvancouver.com First week of August. A massive party around the West End and Sunset Beach on English Bay. At the same time is **Out on Screen Queer Film Festival**, www.outonscreen.com

## Helpline

**Gay and Lesbian Centre Helpline**: T 6846869.

## Magazines and newspapers

**XtraWest**, T 6849696, www.xtra.ca The best place to find out what's going on. Published every other Wednesday and widely available around the West End.

## Organizations

**Gay and Lesbian Centre**, 1170 Bute St, T 6845307. *Map 2, E5, p250* Programmes, services, information and support, discussion groups, clinics, etc. Also houses *Out on the Shelves Library*.

**Gay and Lesbian Business Association of Greater Vancouver**, 720-999 W Broadway, T 7394522. Check out their directory at www.glba.org

## Saunas

**Club Vancouver**, 339 W Pender, **T** 6815719. *Map 3, E3, p252* The raunchier option. Blackout nights, lunch-time specials and so on.

**Fahrenheit 212**, 1048 Davie, **T** 6899719. *Map 2, F6, p250* More upmarket than most, with jacuzzis, lounges, music, etc.

**Hastings Steam and Sauna**, 766 E Hastings, **T** 2515455. *Map 1, G4, p249* Friendly and mostly straight, with a more cruisy area downstairs. Popular with those in the know.

## Websites

**www.gaycanada.com** For general information and links.
**www.purpleroofs.com** Excellent for listings of all kinds of gay-friendly businesses across the country.

West Coast folk are relaxed in their attitude towards children and, with so many parks, gardens and green spaces to explore, Vancouver is a very child-friendly city. As well as some of the world's biggest trees, Stanley Park in particular has plenty of activities grouped around the Aquarium, and the whole Granville Island/Vanier Park/Kits Beach area has much to offer. Kids are equally likely to enjoy walks in Lighthouse Park, the SkyRide to Grouse Mountain and the dramatic Capilano Suspension Bridge. In summer, beaches are a favourite. Those around Point Grey are some of the least crowded and most suitable for families, especially Spanish Banks which has warm, shallow water ideal for paddling. A good number of sights are specifically aimed at children, such as Science World, and most of the adult-oriented sights make an effort to entertain them too. Victoria also has a wealth of attractions for kids. If it's the outdoors you're after, children usually learn to ski a lot faster than adults, and they'll enjoy other activities too, such as tobogganing, ice skating, snow tubing or even a gentle canoe trip up Indian Arm.

# Vancouver

## Sights

**Vancouver Aquarium Marine Science Centre**, Avison Way, Stanley Park, **T** 6593474, www.vanaqua.org  *Daily 1000-1730, summer 0930-1900. $14.95, $11.95 concessions, $8.95 children, under 3s free. Bus No 135 from Hastings. A free shuttle bus runs around the park in summer.  Map 4, D6, p254  See also p48*  A fantastic place for kids of all ages. Entertainment is provided by dolphins, seals, otters and those mesmerizing white beluga whales. There are many other weird, wonderful and colourful creatures to observe, including giant Pacific octopuses, corals, anemones, jellyfish and a large collection of exotic frogs. In the *Tropical* and *Amazon* galleries are such favourites as snakes, caymans, anacondas and assorted lizards. Nearby in Stanley Park are a playground, a **Water Park**, a **Miniature Railway** and **Children's Farmyard**. *Both open daily 1100-1600 Apr-Sep, weekends only Oct-Mar, each $4, $3 senios, $2 children.*

**Science World**, 1455 Quebec St, **T** 4437440, www.science world.bc.ca  *Mon-Fri 1000-1700, Sat-Sun 1000-1800. $12.75, $8.50 concessions; $17.75, $13.50 concessions with Omnimax; $13.50, $10.50 concessions for Omnimax double bill. SkyTrain; False Creek Ferry; Bus No 3 or 8 on Granville or Hastings, No 19 on Pender, all three on Main.  Map 3, I5, p253  See also p39*  Though adults will also relish the experience, Science World is essentially for kids, who will be transfixed from the moment they see that bizarre moving sculpture outside. The Main Gallery on Level 2 is packed with fun, hands-on exhibits that will delight and confound. You can blow square bubbles, play piano with your feet like Tom Hanks in *Big*, watch your shadow freeze on the wall, and get engrossed in all kinds of mind-benders, puzzles and games. The Kidspace Gallery has interactive stuff aimed at younger children. Fun scientific demonstrations take place periodically on the Centre Stage and there are shows for older kids in the High-Definition Science Theatre. The Alcan Omnimax theatre has the largest domed screen in the world.

**Granville Island Sport Fishing, Model Ships and Model Trains Museums**, 1502 Duranleau St, **T** 6831939, www.sportfishingmuseum.ca, www.modelshipsmuseum.ca, www.modeltrainsmuseum.ca *Daily 1000-1730. $6.50, $5 senior, $3.50. Map 2, J4, p251 See also p52* These three museums rolled into one are highly recommended for kids with even a passing interest in models. The collection of model and toy trains includes an extensive working railway that runs through a classic British Columbia landscape on four levels. But the highlight is the extraordinary collection of giant model ships and submarines, including a few that were used to make films and TV series. Nearby is the Kids' Market (see p198 and p224), and a **Water Park**.

**HR MacMillan Space Centre**, 1100 Chestnut St, Vanier Park, **T** T7387827, www.hrmacmillanspacecentre.com *Daily 1000-1700, closed Mon Sep-Jun. $12.75, $9.75 concessions, $8.75 children, under 5s free. Bus No 2 or 22 from Burrard, then walk, or ferry from the Aquatic Centre. Map 2, H2, p251 See also p52* Kids will enjoy the funky crab fountain outside, but don't drag them round the Vancouver Museum. This place is much more fun. It's mainly aimed at older children, who can learn all about the Earth's geological composition, the nature of life in space and the logistics of space travel. There are science demonstrations dotted with wacky experiments, a planetarium, and 15-minute rides on the exciting Virtual Voyages Simulator.

**Maritime Museum**, 1905 Ogden Av, Vanier Park, **T** 2578300, www.vmm.bc.ca *Tue-Sat 1000-1700, Sun 1200-1700. $8, $5.50 concessions, under 5s free. Bus No 2 or 22 from Burrard, then walk, or ferry from the Aquatic Centre. Map 2, G1, p251. See also p53* Aimed

Kids

### The sweet side of town

*Indiatown, or the Punjabi Market, is the place to go for handmade sweets, all-you-can-eat buffets, gold, saris and a lavish Sikh Temple.*

primarily at adults, this museum will certainly appeal to kids who like such things. There are some fun exhibits on pirates for instance, and a hands-on area for younger kids.

**Playland Amusement Park**, Pacific National Exhibition grounds in Hastings Park, **T** 2532311. *Bus No 4, 10 or 16 north on Granville. Daily mid-Jun to early-Sep, and weekends from Apr. Map 1, G5, p249* One of the biggest and longest-running fairgrounds in the country, with 40 or so exciting rides.

### Day care centres

**Westcoast Child Care Resource Centre**, **T** 7095699, www.wstcoast.org If you need to leave your kids in care for a day or two, make a call in advance to the referral line.

Kids

**Crabtree Corner**, **T** 6892808. This is the only other centre that may accommodate you, but spaces are limited.

## Eating

**Earl's**, 1185 Robson, **T** 6690020. *Map 2, D7, p250* and 1601 W Broadway, **T** 7365663. *Map 5, E8, p255*. Canadians love their 'family-style' restaurants and, with a couple of branches in Vancouver, this is by far the best of them. Particularly colourful, fun environments for kids.

## Shopping

**Kids' Market**, 1496 Cartwright St, Granville Island, **T** 6898447. *Map 2, K4, p251* Contains 25 stores just for children, many selling locally handmade toys and clothes.

**The Toybox**, 3002 W Broadway, **T** 7384322. *Map 5, E3, p255* A friendly, well-organized shop full of toys, puzzles and games.

Directory

## Airline offices

**Air Canada**, **T** 1888-2472262. **Air Transat**, **T** 1877-8726728.
**American**, **T** 1800-4337300. **British Airways**, **T** 1800-2479297.
**Continental**, **T** 1800-2310856. **KLM**, **T** 1800-3615073.
**Lufthansa**, **T** 1800-5635954. **Qantas**, **T** 1800-2274500. **Westjet**,
**T** 1800-5385696.

## Banks and ATMs

The main Canadian banks are clustered in a few blocks around
Burrard and Georgia. **CIBC**, 400 Burrard, **T** 1800-4652422; **HSBC**,
885 W Georgia, **T** 1888-3104722; **National Bank of Canada**, 555
Burrard, **T** 6615500; **Royal Bank**, 1025 W Georgia,
**T** 1800-7692511; **Scotiabank**, 650 W Georgia, **T** 6682094; **TD
Bank**, 701 W Georgia, **T** 6890611. For currency exchange: **Benny
Lee**, 619 W Hastings, **T** 6834241; **Citizens Bank of Canada**, 815
W Hastings, **T** 7087877; **Custom House**, 375 Water St, **T** 4826000;
**Inter Currency**, 609 W Hastings, **T** 6888668; **Money Mart**,
www.moneymart.ca have branches all over the city, including
1281 Howe, 498 W Broadway, 1895 Commercial, 199 W Hastings,
and 24-hour at 345 E Broadway and 1195 Davie; **Moneywise**, 819
Davie, **T** 4082274; **Thomas Cook Foreign Exchange**, 130-999
Canada Place, **T** 6411229.

## Bicycle hire

**Bike Cellar**, 1856 W 4th, **T** 7387167; **Deep Cove Bikes**, 4310
Gallant Av, **T** 9291918; **Simon's Bike Shop**, 608 Robson,
**T** 6021181; **Spokes Bicycle Rentals**, 1798 W Georgia St,
**T** 6885141. In **Tofino**: **Fibre Options**, Campbell/4th, **T** 7252192.

## Car hire

All the major rental agencies have offices in the indoor car park at
the airport and Downtown. **Avis**, 757 Hornby, **T** 6062869; **Budget**,
501 W Georgia, **T** 6687000; **Hertz**, 1128 Seymour, **T** 6064711;
**Thrifty**, 1015 Burrard, **T** 6061666. Prices start at about $40 per day,

$200 per week, $800 per month plus tax and insurance. A mini-van from **Rent-a-wreck**, 1349 Hornby, **T** 6880001, works out at about $590 per week all-inclusive. The expensive but luxurious choice is to rent an RV from **Cruise Canada**, **T** 9465775, www.cruise canada.com, or **Go West**, **T** 9875288, www.go-west.com Prices start at about $145 per day for a small unit, $193 per day for a 24-footer, plus tax and insurance.

## Chemists
See under Pharmacies.

## Consulates
**Australia**, 1225-888 Dunsmuir, **T** 6841177. **Belgium**, 570-688 W Hastings, **T** 6846838. **Denmark**, 755-777 Hornby, **T** 6845171. **Germany**, 704-999 Canada Pl, **T** 6848377. **Italy**, 1100-510 W Hastings, **T** 6847288. **Japan**, 900-1177 W Hastings, **T** 6845868. **Netherlands**, 473 Howe, **T** 6846448. **New Zealand**, 1200-888 Dunsmuir, **T** 6847388. **Norway**, 200 Burrard, **T** 6827977. **Sweden**, 1100-1188 W Georgia, **T** 6835838. **Switzerland**, 790-999 Canada Place, **T** 6842231. **UK**, 800-1111 Melville, **T** 6834421. **US**, 1075-1095 W Pender, **T** 6854311, 24-hour visa information for US citizens, **T** 1900-4512778.

## Credit card lines
**VISA**, **T** 1800-3368472; **Mastercard**, **T** 1800-3613361.

## Cultural institutions
**Vancouver Francophone Cultural Centre**, 1551 W 7th Av, **T** 7369806.

## Dentists
**Association of Dental Surgeons of BC**, **T** 7367202. **Acute Medical Dental Centre**, 2561 Commercial Dr, **T** 8770664 (24-hour). Walk-in clinic.

## Disabled

With more than 14,000 sidewalk ramps, Vancouver claims to be one of the most wheelchair-accessible cities in the world. Half of the buses and all but the Granville St SkyTrain station are wheelchair accessible and the HandyDART is a bus service designed for wheelchair users. It mainly runs 0630-1900 weekdays, and can be booked at **T** 4302692. For information call **T** 4302892. Vancouver Airport was designed to be friendly to those with hearing, visual and mobility difficulties. For accessible taxis call **Vancouver Taxi**, **T** 2555111. To rent a lift-equipped van call the **BC Paraplegic Association**, T3243611. **Pacific Lines** service to Victoria is wheelchair accessible. For a list of hotels with wheel-in showers contact **We're Accessible**, **T** 7312197.

## Electricity

The current in Canada is 110V AC, 60 cycle. Plugs have two flat parallel prongs and sometimes a third that is cylindrical.

## Embassies

See under Consulates.

## Emergency numbers

For all emergencies, **T** 911. **Fire and rescue**, 1090 Haro (Downtown), **T** 6656007; 199 Main, **T** 6656002; 1001 Nicola (West End), **T** 6656006. **24-hour Crisis Centre**, **T** 8723311.

## Hospitals and clinics

**Vancouver General**, 855 W 12th St, **T** 8754111. **St Paul's**, 1081 Burrard, **T** 6822344. **Broadway and Burrard**, 1816 W Broadway, **T** 7361888. *0900-2100*. **Care-Point Medical Centres**, **T** 8781000, www.CarePoint.bc.ca, 1623 Commercial Dr; 1125 Davie; 1175 Denman. *Mon-Fri 0900-2100, Sat-Sun 0900-1800*. **Chinatown Centre**, 165-288 E Georgia, **T** 6053382. Walk-in clinic with acupuncture and traditional Chinese medicine. **Health Care**,

2590 Commercial Dr, **T** 8711535. **Integral Chinese Therapy Centre**, 105-1956 W Broadway, **T** 7328968. **Khatsahlano**, 2689 W Broadway, **T** 7319187. *0900-2045*. **Medicentre**, Bentall Centre, 1055 Dunsmuir, **T** 6838138.

## Internet/email
**Cyberia**, 1284 Robson, **T** 6331477. Open 24 hours, $4 per hour or $20 per 10 hours. **Cyber Space**, 1451 Robson, **T** 6846004. **Dakoda's**, 1602 Yew St, Kitsilano, **T** 7315616. **Soapy's**, 141-757 W Hastings, **T** 6891909. **Westend Bay**, 1168 Denman. $10 per five hours. **Central Library**, 350 W Georgia. $2.50 per 30 mins.

## Left luggage
**Airport**, **T** 3034519. **Bus station**, lockers.

## Libraries
**Vancouver Public Central Library**, 350 W Georgia, **T** 3313600. Useful branches are at 2425 MacDonald (Kitsilano), **T** 6653976; 370 E Broadway, **T** 6653962; 870 Denman, **T** 6653972 (West End).

## Lost property
**TransLink**, **T** 6827887; **Airport**, **T** 2766104; **Police**, **T** 6652232.

## Media
The **Globe and Mail** is Canada's main broadsheet; the **Vancouver Sun**, **National Post** and **Province** are fairly trashy tabloids. **Macleans** is a Canadian equivalent of **Time** magazine, which also has a slightly modified Canadian version. **Equinox** and **Canadian Geographic** are well-respected nature publications. **Adbusters** is a well put-together anti-corporate magazine published in Vancouver. **CBC Radio** is the easiest way to get a grip on the Canadian psyche. The best range of magazines and international newspapers are found at **The Great Canadian News Co**, 1092 Robson; and **Does Your Mother Know?**, 2139 W 4th Av.

## Motorcycle hire

**Adventure Tours @ Explore BC!**, 1528 Duranleau, Granville Island, **T** 7200155; **Royal Pacific Executive Rentals**, 1820 Burrard, **T** 7308332.

## Pharmacies

**London Drugs** has branches at 70 Granville, 1187 Robson and 1650 Davie. **Shoppers Drug Mart** has branches at the Pacific Centre at 700 Georgia, and 1020 Denman. Also handy are **Gastown Pharmacy**, 288 Carrall; **Kripps Pharmacy**, 994 Granville; **Pharmasave**, 1160 Burrard.

## Police

916 Granville, **T** 7172920; 1122 Bute/Davie, **T** 7172924; 200 Burrard, **T** 7172916; 870 Denman, **T** 8996250; 219 Abbott, **T** 7172929. See also under Emergency numbers.

## Post offices

**Main Post Office** with General Delivery (Poste Restante): 395 W Georgia, **T** 6625722. Others are at 595 Burrard St; 523 Main; 732 Davie. Letters can be posted at most major pharmacies.

## Public holidays

New Year's Day; Good Friday; Easter Monday; Victoria Day (third Monday in May); Canada Day (1 July); British Columbia Day (first Monday in August); Labour Day (first Monday in September); Thanksgiving (second Monday in October); Remembrance Day (11 November); Christmas Day; Boxing Day.

## Religious services

**Anglican**, Christ Church Anglican Cathedral, 690 Burrard; St James Anglican Church, 303 E Cordova; **Baptist**, First Baptist Church, 969 Burrard; **Buddhist**, PTT Buddhist Society, 514 Keefer, **T** 2553811; **Catholic**, Holy Rosary Catholic Cathedral, 646 Richards; **Hindu**,

Hindu Temple, 3885 Albert, Burnaby; **Islamic**, Islamic Information Centre, 3127 Kingsway; **Sikh**, Sikh Temple, 8000 Ross.

## Taxis
**Yellow Cab Co**, T 6811111. **Black Top/Checker Cabs**, T 1800-4941111.

## Telephone
**Operator**, T 0. **IDD**, T 011. **Dialling codes**  Long-distance calls within Canada have to be preceded by 1 then the 3-digit code, T 604 for Vancouver and surroundings, T 250 for the rest of BC. Public phones are numerous and take coins and credit cards. Local calls are free from personal phones, but there's a charge of 35c at pay phones for an unlimited amount of time. Any long distance numbers beginning with T 800, 888, 877 or 777 are free in North America. There is no charge for calling T 411 for directory enquiries, or T 911 for police and emergencies. Long-distance and international calls are cheaper with a call-card available from newsagents and gas stations.

## Time
Pacific Time is eight hours behind Greenwich Mean Time.

## Toilets
Public toilets in Vancouver are almost extinct except in stations and shopping centres. All places selling food are required by law to have a washroom.

## Transport enquiries
**Vancouver International Airport** (YVR), T 2077077, www.yvr.ca  **Greyhound**, T 1800-6618747, www.greyhound.ca **Pacific Coach Lines**, T 1800-6611725, www.pacificcoach.com For local transport, contact **TransLink**, T 5210400, www.translink.bc.ca  **Amtrak**, T 1800-8727245, www.amtrak.com, for train

## Travel agents and tour operators

**Flight Centre**, T 6069000, T 1888-9675331, have about 17 branches, including: 1232 Davie; 909 Denman; 2194 W 4th; 1050 W Georgia; 655 W Pender; 610 Robson. **Travel Cuts** are at: 567 Seymour St, T 6592830; 120 W Broadway, T 6592887; and Granville Island, T 6592820. **Hagen's**, 204-1789 Davie, T 2572088, is a reliable choice. For adventure travel there's **Fresh Tracks**, 1847 W 4th, T 7377880.

In Victoria: **Eagle Wing**, T 3919337, and **Springtide**, T 8836722, www.springtidecharters.com, run whale-watching tours. **Coastline Eco-Tours**, T 5958668, www.coastlinetours.com, run biking, sailing and hiking tours, including a half-day cycling tour of the city for $65. **Vancouver Island Canoe and Kayak Centre**, 575 Pembroke, T 3619365, do canoe and kayak tours. **Nature Calls Eco-tours**, 12 Falstaff Place, T 1877-3614453, organize hiking trips. **Gray Line**, T 3885248, and **Royal Blue Line**, T 3602249, use double-deckers imported from England for their narrated tours of town. **Victoria Harbour Ferry**, T 7080201, run regular 45-minute narrated harbour tours and 50-minute narrated gorge tours.

Background

# A sprint through history

**8,000 BC**  The earliest remains of human habitation in the Vancouver area date back some 10,000 years.

**200 BC**  The Marpole civilization flourishes. Living in large cedar plank houses and navigating in dugout canoes, they produce superb stone carvings and copper ornaments.

**1770**  Spanish navigator José María Narvaez ventures into the Georgia Strait. Spanish, Russian, British, Dutch and French explorers arrive on the West Coast seeking the elusive Northwest Passage, a northern trade route to the Orient.

**1771**  Captain George Vancouver (former apprentice to James Cook) and the Spaniard Dionisio Alcalá Galiano both sail into Burrard Inlet. The Englishman spends just one day in the city that will bear his name. The area is mostly inhabited by the Squamish and the Musqueam.

**1827**  The fur-trading Hudson's Bay Company establishes Fort Langley on the southeastern outskirts of today's Greater Vancouver.

**1832**  2,000 beaver pelts are shipped from the fort.

**1840s**  Vancouver becomes the biggest exporter of salted salmon on the coast.

**1858**  Gold is discovered on the Fraser River. The arrival of 25,000 prospectors sparks fears of American expansion and the governor of Vancouver Island in Victoria declares the mainland a British colony. The magnificent giant trees that cover the whole area are chopped down at an alarming rate; there is also a sharp decline in the number of local Natives.

**1867** The area then known as Granville evolved around Vancouver's first major industry, Hastings Mill. It was nicknamed Gastown after 'Gassy' Jack Leighton, garrulous owner of its first saloon (see p39).

**1871** BC agrees to join the new Confederation of Canada on condition that a railway will be built to connect east and west. Two months later the 'Great Fire' destroys the ramshackle town in less than an hour, but rebuilding (this time in brick) begins before the embers have stopped smoking.

**1875** The town's population has swollen from 400 to 13,000. It doubles again in the next decade.

**1887** Electricity reaches Vancouver.

**1911-1929** By 1911 the population has reached over 120,000 and is doubling every five years. A period of untrammelled development (reflected by a series of buildings that replace each other as the tallest in the British Empire) only comes to an end with the Wall Street Crash of 1929.

**Mid-1960s** Downtown rejuvenation programme brings the Robson Square complex, BC Place, renovation of Gastown and pedestrianization of Granville Street.

**1986** The city celebrates its 100th anniversary by hosting Expo '86, which attracts over 21 million visitors and leads to a new wave of development and the construction of many landmark buildings such as

Canada Place and the distinctive futuristic sphere of Science World.

**2001-2002**  BC's right-wing premier Gordon Campbell cuts taxes then uses financial deficits as an excuse to cut just about every service, benefit and facility in the province. Larry Campbell, no relation and at the other end of the political spectrum, becomes Vancouver's mayor. A former coroner, he has vowed in particular to address the issue of drugs, homelessness and squalor in Downtown's East Side.

# Art and architecture

**Up to AD 1827**  Local Native groups live in large cedar plank longhouses; the men create carvings from wood, stone, copper, bone, horn, leather, ivory and shell, including spectacular large-scale works in red cedar, such as totem poles, house posts and canoes. Women weave practical but beautiful textiles. Check out the online digital gallery of Native art at www.lights.com/sicc2/keepinghouse

**1871**  After the 'Great Fire', Gastown is rebuilt in cut stone and brick, with heavy timbers for columns and rafters. Styles are predominantly European, with many Italianate details.

**1897-1925**  Francis Rattenbury designs the Vancouver Courthouse (later transformed into the Vancouver Art Gallery) and almost all of Victoria's grand, turn-of-the-century constructions, including the *Empress Hotel* and Parliament Building. His classical, British style offers little originality, but brings a new level of sophistication to building technology and craftsmanship.

**1900-1945**  At a time when nobody else seems to recognize the beauty and significance of Native Canadian art and architecture, Victoria-born artist Emily Carr tours aboriginal sites that will soon fall into complete neglect, painting the ancient villages, longhouses and totem poles. Success eludes her until, at the age of 57, she is invited to exhibit in Eastern Canada. She begins to receive the kind of exposure and recognition she deserves. Large collections of her work are held at both the Vancouver and Victoria Art Galleries, and her Victoria house can also be visited.

**1920-1960**  Largely due to the talents of architect Ned Pratt, the firm of Thompson Berwick Pratt train and inspire a whole generation of architects who start moving towards a distinctive BC style. The culmination of such progress takes the shape of Ron Thom, who succeeds in combining the horizontal style of Frank Lloyd Wright with the demands of the West Coast climate.

**1950s-90s**  Vancouver-born Bill Reid starts investigating the arts of the Haida of Haida Gwaii (Queen Charlotte Islands). He goes on to become the most important Native American artist of the 20th century. See p58. In his wake, Native art is enjoying a resurgence, covering the full spectrum from commercial and often trashy tourist kitsch to traditional artworks.

**1960s-70s**  Arthur Erickson invents a style of architecture that is unique to Vancouver. He has many key buildings dotted around town, including the Art Gallery and Sikh Temple. His buildings blend into the landscape and, in keeping with the frequently overcast climate of the West Coast, he is famous for creating dramatic structures out of potentially dull, mute colours, and concrete and glass canopies. His structures are also designed to make a statement about their purpose, as demonstrated by the Native Big House design of the UBC Museum of

Anthropology (1973-76), and the deliberate openness of the Law Courts complex at Robson Square (1976).

**1960s-2003** A whole generation of Vancouver-born or bred artists start to gain national and international recognition such as Ian Wallace, best known for his conceptual art, painting and photographic murals; Jeff Wall, famed as much for his theoretical writing as for his large-scale, back-lit cibachrome photographs, which often allude to the history of art and problems of representation; associated artist Rodney Graham, whose work tends to 'annex' itself to existing works of various media, including sculpture, literature and music; Liz Mager has gained renown for her installations and multimedia works, and the social, cultural and political questions they raise.

**2003** No single architect dominates the current scene, and building styles have become radically more eclectic. The 21st-century Vancouver edifice par excellence is the sleek, towering skyscraper whose surface is almost entirely composed of giant sheets of glass: 'see-throughs' as Douglas Coupland calls them.

# Books

Canada produced many first-rate and internationally successful writers in the 20th century, including **Margaret Atwood**: *The Robber Bride* (1993); *Alias Grace* (1996) and *The Blind Assassin* (2000); **Robertson Davies**: *Fifth Business* (1970), *The Rebel Angels* (1981), *What's Bred in the Bone* (1985); **Alice Munro**: *Who Do You Think You Are?* (1978); **Michael Ondaatje**: *In the Skin of a Lion* (1987); *The English Patient* (1992); *Anil's Ghost* (2000); **Jane Urquhart**: *Away* (1993), *The Underpainter* (1997); **Carol Sheilds**: *The Stone Diaries* (1993); **Rohinton Mistry**: *A Fine Balance* (1995); and winner of the 2002 Booker Prize, **Yann Martel**: *Life of Pi* (2002). All of these are useful for understanding the Canadian psyche, but none comes from British Columbia.

The following have a greater bearing on the Vancouver area: **Coupland, Douglas**, *Generation X: Tales for an Accelerated Culture* (1991), Douglas & MacIntyre. Probably the most famous novel written by a Vancouverite, this came to crystallize the entire post-boomer generation. Recently Coupland put together an interesting book of anecdotes and photos concerning Vancouver, *City of Glass* (2001). In *Souvenir of Canada* (2002) he gave the same treatment of quirky pictures and observant witticisms to the country as a whole.

**Hodgins, Jack**, *The Resurrection of Joseph Bourne* (1979), Macmillan. All of Hodgkins' novels deal with characters reconstructed from his Vancouver Island childhood. Eccentric but realistic, they are West Coast archetypes, placed in life-affirming situations and treated with stylistic suppleness in narratives that are playful and sometimes experimental.

**Johnson, E Pauline**, *Legends of Vancouver* (1911), Quarry Press. A timeless collection of stories written by this celebrated Native poet, and based on legends recounted to her by Chief Joe Capilano.

**King, Thomas**, *Green Grass, Running Water* (1993), Harper Collins. The best-known of Canada's First Nations authors, King writes with great wit and narrative ease. Also recommended is his collection of short stories, *One Good Story, That One* (1993). He has also edited *All My Relations* (1990), an anthology of Native Canadian fiction.

**Love, Karen (Ed)**, *Facing History: Portraits from Vancouver* (2002), Arsenal Pulp Press. A brand new collection of interesting photos and essays about the city, that knocks the socks off anything else in a similar vein.

**McClelland and Stewart**, *Selected Poems 1961-92, George Bowering* (1993). A good overview of the vast body of work of this renowned Vancouverite who has just been named Canada's first ever Poet Laureate. *Burning Water* (1980), also by Bowering, is a fine account of George Vancouver's voyages.

**Pistolesi, Andrea**, *Vancouver: Sunrise to Sunset (1998)*, Bonechi. Best collection of glossy photos depicting this photogenic city.

**Stouck, D & Wilkinson, M** (Ed), *West by Northwest: BC Short Stories* (1998), Polestar. A collection of short modern fiction by BC writers.

**Vogel, A & Wyse, D**, *Vancouver: A History in Photos* (1993), Altitude. A visual approach to the city's past, captured in vintage black and white.

**Wilson, Ethel**, *Swamp Angel* (1954), McClelland & Stewart. Born in South Africa, Wilson came to live in Vancouver, becoming one of the first Canadian writers to truly capture the rugged and unsurpassed beauty of the BC landscape. Unpretentious and lucid, her style is typified by this strong sense of place.

# Index

# Credits

**Footprint credits**

Text editor: Felicity Laughton
Series editor: Rachel Fielding

Production: Jo Morgan, Mark Thomas
Davina Rungasamy
In-house cartography: Claire Benison,
Kevin Feeney, Robert Lunn,
Sarah Sorensen
Proofreading: Elizabeth Barrick

Design: Mytton Williams
Maps: PCGraphics (UK) Ltd
Colour map: Robert Lunn

**Photography credits**

Front cover: Alamy
Inside: Alison Bigg
Generic images: John Matchett
Back cover: Alison Bigg

**Print**

Manufactured in Italy by LegoPrint

**Publishing information**

Footprint Vancouver
1st edition
Text and maps © Footprint Handbooks
March 2003

ISBN 1 903471 65 6
CIP DATA: a catalogue record for this
book is available from the British Library

® Footprint Handbooks and the Footprint
mark are a registered trademark of
Footprint Handbooks Ltd

Published by Footprint Handbooks
6 Riverside Court
Lower Bristol Road
Bath, BA2 3DZ, UK
T +44 (0)1225 469141
F +44 (0)1225 469461
E discover@footprintbooks.com
W www.footprintbooks.com

Distributed in the USA by
Publishers Group West

# Complete title list

## Latin America & Caribbean

Argentina
Barbados (P)
Bolivia
Brazil
Caribbean Islands
Central America & Mexico
Chile
Colombia
Costa Rica
Cuba
Cusco & the Inca Trail
Dominican Republic
Ecuador & Galápagos Handbook
Guatemala Handbook
Havana (P)
Mexico
Nicaragua
Peru
Rio de Janeiro
South American Handbook
Venezuela

## North America

Vancouver (P)
Western Canada

## Africa

Cape Town (P)
East Africa
Libya
Marrakech & the High Atlas
Morocco
Namibia
South Africa
Tunisia
Uganda

## Middle East

Egypt
Israel
Jordan
Syria & Lebanon

## Asia

Bali
Bangkok & the Beaches
Cambodia
Goa
India
Indian Himalaya
Indonesia
Laos
Malaysia
Myanmar (Burma)
Nepal
Pakistan
Rajasthan & Gujarat
Singapore
South India
Sri Lanka
Sumatra
Thailand
Tibet
Vietnam

## Australasia

Australia
New Zealand
Sydney (P)
West Coast Australia

## Europe

Andalucía
Barcelona
Berlin (P)
Bilbao (P)
Bologna (P)
Copenhagen (P)
Croatia
Dublin (P)
Edinburgh (P)
England
Glasgow
Ireland
London
Madrid (P)
Naples (P)
Northern Spain
Paris (P)
Reykjavik (P)
Scotland
Scotland Highlands & Islands
Spain
Turkey

(P) denotes pocket Handbook

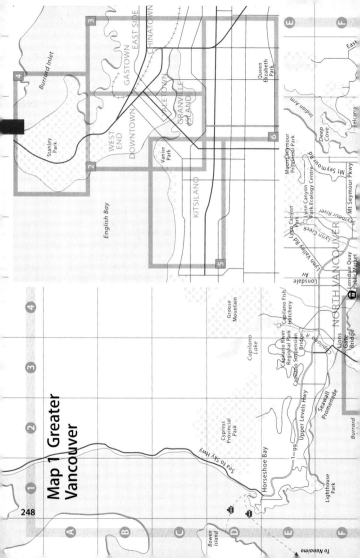

# Map 1 Greater Vancouver

248

Bowen Island

To Nanaimo

Horseshoe Bay

Cypress Provincial Park

Sea to Sky Hwy

Grouse Mountain

Capilano Lake

Capilano River Regional Park

Capilano Fish Hatchery

Capilano Suspension Bridge

Upper Levels Hwy

I-99

Lions Gate Bridge

Seawall Promenade

Lighthouse Park

NORTH VANCOUVER

Lonsdale Av

Lonsdale Quay Public Market

Capilano Rd

Burrard Inlet

Stanley Park

English Bay

Burrard

WEST END

DOWNTOWN

GASTOWN

EAST SIDE

CHINATOWN

YALETOWN

GRANVILLE ISLAND

Vanier Park

KITSILANO

Queen Elizabeth Park

Lynn Valley Rd

Lynn Canyon Park

Lynn Canyon Park Ecology Centre

Lynn Creek

Lynn Canyon

Seymour River

Mount Seymour Provincial Park

Mt Seymour Pkwy

Mt Seymour Rd

Indian Arm

Deep Cove

Belcarra

# Map 2 West End to Downtown

250

DOWNTOWN

WEST END

Stanley Park

Lost Lagoon

Lagoon Dr

Coal Harbour

English Bay

English Bay Beach

**Streets and features:**

Lagoon Dr
Chilco St
Gilford St
Denman St
Cardero St
Nicola St
Broughton St
Jervis St
Bute St
Thurlow St
Burnaby St
Harwood St
Beach Av
Pendrell St
Comox St
Nelson St
Barclay St
Haro St
Robson St
Alberni St
Melville St
Cordova St West
Hastings St West
Pender St West
Georgia St
Bayshore Dr
Bidwell St
Blaine St
Park La

Coal Harbour Seawalk

HOWE ST
HORNBY ST
Smithe St
Robson St
Granville Mall
Dunsmuir St

**Landmarks:**

- Canadian Craft & Design Museum
- Christ Church Cathedral
- Hotel Vancouver
- Vancouver Art Gallery
- Cathedral Place
- HSBC Building
- Robson Square & Courthouse
- King George Hospital
- Barclay Heritage Square
- Roedde House Museum
- St Paul's Hospital
- Orpheum

Burrard S

0 meters 100
0 yards 100

N

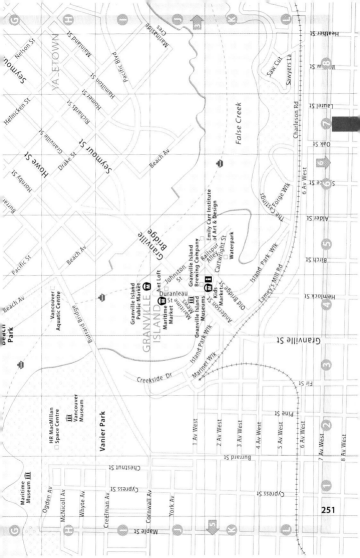

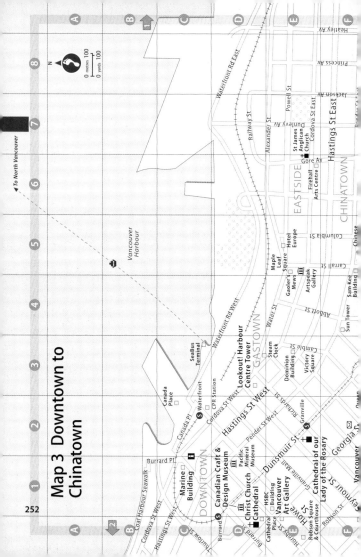

# Map 3 Downtown to Chinatown

To North Vancouver →

N
0 metres 100
0 yards 100

Coal Harbour Seawalk

Vancouver Harbour

Canada Place

SeaBus Terminal

Waterfront Rd West

Waterfront Rd East

CPR Station

Cordova St West

Waterfront

Railway St

Alexander St

Powell St

Heatley Av

Princess Av

Jackson Av

DOWNTOWN

Burrard Pl

Marine Building

Canadian Craft & Design Museum

Pacific Mineral Museum

Lookout! Harbour Centre Tower

GASTOWN

Water St

Dunlevy Av

Cordova St East

St James Anglican Church

Gore Av

Firehall Arts Centre

EASTSIDE

Hastings St East

Hastings St West

Steam Clock

Gamble St

Maple Leaf Square

Hotel Europe

Columbia St

Chinese

CHINATOWN

Christ Church Cathedral

Dominion Building

Victory Square

Abbott St

Gaoler's Mews

Artspeak Gallery

Carrall St

Sam Kee Building

HSBC Building

Vancouver Art Gallery

Cathedral Place

Pender St West

Dunsmuir St

Sun Tower

Cathedral of our Lady of the Rosary

Robson Square & Courthouse

Georgia St

Vancouver St

Seymour St

Howe St

Granville Mall

Richards St

Robson St

Burrard St

Thurlow St

Hornby St

Queen

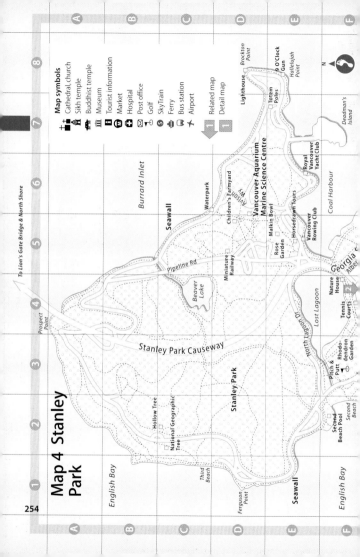

# Map 4 Stanley Park

**Map symbols**

- ✠ Cathedral, church
- ☬ Sikh temple
- 卍 Buddhist temple
- 🏛 Museum
- ❓ Tourist information
- 🛒 Market
- ✚ Hospital
- ✉ Post office
- Ⓢ SkyTrain
- ⛴ Ferry
- 🚌 Bus station
- ✈ Airport

▭ Related map

▮ Detail map

To Lion's Gate Bridge & North Shore

Burrard Inlet

Seawall

Pipeline Rd

Beaver Lake

Stanley Park Causeway

Prospect Point

Hollow Tree

National Geographic Tree

Third Beach

Ferguson Point

English Bay

Stanley Park

Seawall

Second Beach Pool

Second Beach

English Bay

Waterpark

Miniature Railway

Children's Farmyard

Malkin Bowl

Rose Garden

Vancouver Aquarium Marine Science Centre

Horsedrawn Tours

Vancouver Rowing Club

Royal Vancouver Yacht Club

Coal Harbour

Georgia

Alber

North Lagoon Dr

Lost Lagoon

Nature House

Tennis Courts

Pitch & Putt

Rhododendron Garden

Lighthouse

Brockton Point

9 O'Clock Gun

Hallelujah Point

Totem Poles

Deadman's Island

N

# Map 5 Kitsilano

255

# Map 6 South Vancouver